The Literary Trail
of Greater Boston

The Literary Trail
of Greater Boston

Susan Wilson
for the Boston History Collaborative

Revised Edition

Commonwealth Editions
Beverly, Massachusetts

In loving memory of Murphy Brown Wilson
and for my family, Rebecca, Otto, and Gilda

First edition published by Houghton Mifflin Company, 2000, ISBN 0-618-05013-2

ISBN-13: 978-1-889833-67-5
ISBN-10: 1-889833-67-3

Library of Congress Cataloging-in-Publication Data
Wilson, Susan (Susan Carolyn)
 The literary trail of greater Boston : a tour of sites in Boston, Cambridge, and Concord /
Susan Wilson for the Boston History Collaborative.-- Rev. ed.
  p. cm.
 Includes bibliographical references and index.
 ISBN 1-889833-67-3
 1. Literary landmarks--Massachusetts--Boston--Guidebooks. 2. Literary landmarks--
Massachusetts--Concord--Guidebooks.. 3. Literary landmarks--Massachusetts--
Cambridge--Guidebooks. 4. American literature--Massachusetts--Boston--History and
criticism. 5. American literature--Massachusetts--Concord--History and criticism. 6.
American literature--Massachusetts--Cambridge--History and criticism. 7. Authors,
American--Homes and haunts--Massachusetts--Guidebooks. 8. Cambridge (Mass.)--
Intellectual life. 9. Concord (Mass.)--Intellectual life. 10. Boston (Mass.)--Intellectual life.
I. Boston History Collaborative. II. Title.
 PS144.B67W55 2005
 810.9'974461--dc22   2005002280

First-edition cover design by Christopher Moisan,
adapted by Anne Lenihan Rolland
Original maps by Bruce C . Jones
Interior design by Laura McFadden
Layout by Anne Lenihan Rolland

Printed in the United States

Commonwealth Editions
266 Cabot Street, Beverly, Massachusetts 01915
www.commonwealtheditions.com

Visit The Literary Trail of Greater Boston at www.literarytrailofgreaterboston.org.

*Cover photographs, clockwise from left: Bronson Alcott's study, Orchard House, Concord, courtesy of
Susan Wilson; Kahlil Gibran, c. 1910, courtesy of Kahlil and Jean Gibran; Louisa May Alcott,
c. 1858, courtesy of Orchard House/The Louisa May Alcott Memorial Association; Robert Lowell,
courtesy of the Boston Public Library, Print Department; African Meetinghouse, courtesy of Susan
Wilson; W. E. B. Du Bois, courtesy of Harvard University; Henry Wadsworth Longfellow and
daughter Edith Longfellow, courtesy of the National Park Service, Longfellow National Historic Site.*

Please see page 187 for other credits.

Contents

Acknowledgments

From 1997 through the present, I have been honored to take part in meetings of the Boston History Collaborative, especially those related to the new Literary Trail of Greater Boston. Having been intimately involved in the ongoing development of two of Boston's classic history walks—the Freedom Trail and the Boston Women's Heritage Trail—I was thrilled to listen to ideas about the Literary Trail emerge, grow, and take shape through group discussion and to add my own experiences whenever possible. It was Bob Krim who proposed the Literary Trail idea in an editorial page article he wrote for the *Boston Globe,* followed by the development of a group in the summer of 1998. Without Bob Krim, the director of the Boston History Collaborative, Lisa Simpson, the first director of the Literary Trail, and Jayne Gordon, cultural historian and guide extraordinaire (now executive director of the Thoreau Society), the first edition of this book would not have been possible.

The original incarnation of the Literary Trail in print form was a pamphlet that appeared in 1999; the second was a full-fledged book, published in 2000 by Houghton Mifflin. Without the support of Terry Heagney, Wendy Strothman, and their colleagues at Houghton—all now moved on to greener pastures—that book would never have existed. When Webster Bull of Commonwealth Editions expressed interested in acquiring and publishing a new, updated, and expanded version for 2005, Houghton graciously provided us with all the relevant electronic files and rights. For the enthusiastic support of Commonwealth Editions and the cooperation of Houghton Mifflin, I am forever grateful.

During the summer of 2004, I was able to look anew at the manuscript, allowing me to edit wording, add research, correct errors, and update information. In an effort to make the text as accurate and current as possible, we sent out portions of the original text to more than forty experts in the field, who provided critical support, archival resources, editing skills, fact-checking, and other information for this new edition.

For the Boston segment of the Literary Trail, our knowledgeable "editors" included Stephen Nonack of the Boston Athenaeum, Margaret Bratschi of Boston by Foot, Henry Lee of the Friends of the Public Garden, Mary Frances O'Brien and Mary Bender of the Boston Public Library, Cecily Miller and Al Maze of Forest Hills Cemetery, Barbara Thibault of the Gibson House, Bill Meikle of Historical Entertainments, Mark Thayer and Joyce Gardella of the Mary Baker Eddy Library, Don Yacovone and Kim Nusco of the Massachusetts Historical Society, Mary Rinehart of the Massachusetts State House, Julie Crockford and Beverly Morgan-Welch of the Museum of Afro-American History, Flavia Cigliano of the Nichols House Museum, Eric Breitkreutz of Historic Boston Incorporated (the Old Corner Bookstore building), Emily Curran and Kristen Sherman of the Old South Meeting House, Reverend Gordon Hugenberger of the Park Street Church, Rima Patel and Dave Ritchie of the Omni Parker House, George Sanborn of the State Transportation Library, Anne von Rosenberg of the William Hickling Prescott House, Mary Smoyer and Polly Kaufman of the Boston Women's Heritage Trail, and Ed Gordon of the New England Chapter of the Victorian Society in America.

In Cambridge, we are indebted to Charles Sullivan of the Cambridge Historical Commission, Hugh Crain of the Cambridge Public Library, Janet Heywood of Mount Auburn Cemetery, Bill Carter and Marvin Hightower of Harvard University, Ellen Shea of the Schlesinger Library at the Radcliffe Institute, and Jim Shea and Nancy Jones of Longfellow National Historical Site.

The Concord portion of the text was updated with the assistance of Tom O'Gorham of the Colonial Inn, Judy Stern of the Concord Museum, Deborah Kreiser-Francis of The Old Manse, Jan Turnquist of Orchard House, Bob Derry and Lou Sideris of Minute Man National Historical Park, Jane Sciacca, Leslie Wilson of the Concord Free Public Library, and Jayne Gordon of the Thoreau Society

Finally, our special thanks to the award-winning writers, all of whom have worked or lived in the Greater Boston area, who agreed to share their words and inspiration in both the original and this brand new volume: Anne Bernays, Henry Louis Gates, Jr., Gish Jen, Justin Kaplan, Jane Langton, David McCullough, Robert Pinsky, Patricia Smith, and the late great Julia Child.

Susan Wilson
Cambridge, Massachusetts
April 2005

Introduction

A s a showcase for the American Revolution, Boston has long been an unparalleled national treasure. Still, 1776 was not the only important date in American history, and native Bostonians like Paul Revere, John Hancock, and Samuel Adams were not its only heroes.

In the century following America's War for Independence, the Greater Boston area experienced a whole new "revolution" and fostered a whole new image—that of cultural center, intellectual hub, and literary mecca. The great arc linking Boston, Cambridge, and Concord, Massachusetts, was the spawning ground for an astonishing number of innovative thinkers, writers, poets, and social activists, whose interests ranged from transcendentalism and abolitionism to women's rights and spiritual enlightenment. Among the heroes of this era were such household names as Louisa May Alcott, Henry David Thoreau, Henry Wadsworth Longfellow, Harriet Beecher Stowe, Ralph Waldo Emerson, William Lloyd Garrison, Nathaniel Hawthorne, and Julia Ward Howe. They came to join a pantheon of native scribes that began with colonial talents like Cotton Mather, Benjamin Franklin, and Phillis Wheatley, and eventually grew to include such contemporary giants as Kahlil Gibran, Willa Cather, Sylvia Plath, Robert Frost, Eugene O'Neill, John Updike, and Doris Kearns Goodwin.

Today, the vibrant literary and political reawakening of nineteenth-century Boston is alive, well, and wonderfully retold along the Literary Trail of Greater Boston. Like the famous Freedom Trail, the Literary Trail links a variety of historic sites. While the Freedom Trail is a walking tour of American Revolutionary landmarks in downtown Boston, the Literary Trail is a lengthier excursion—easy to walk in some areas and, in others, better done by bus, auto, or "T"—connecting homes, gathering places, and landscapes associated with nineteenth-century authors and spotlighting Greater Boston's early and ongoing leadership in America's literary renaissance.

The trail, which includes sites like the Boston Athenaeum, the Longfellow House in Cambridge, and Orchard House in Concord, will place some of America's most beloved authors in the rich, fascinating context of their times. Visitors will come to know not only their books—America's classiest and most enduring classics—but also the bookstores, lectures, and poetry readings that flourish here today.

The Literary Trail: An Overview

The main route of the Literary Trail is a linear, sometimes winding, journey that begins in downtown Boston, continues through Cambridge, then moves out to Concord. It can be taken as a driving tour at your own pace or on Literary Trail buses. When traveling from town to town, and when doing the Concord segment of the route, auto or bus are the easiest method of travel, due to the distances. The Boston and Cambridge segments of the main route are fairly compact (or include three or four compact neighborhoods) and can therefore be walked or driven. Visitors have the option of taking the whole trail, or selecting one town or neighborhood to explore in depth--by car, foot, public transportation, or a combination of all three.

Interspersed throughout this text are several tours called "Off the Beaten Path," which are designed for pedestrian travel due to one-way streets, heavy traffic, or the difficulty of parking near many of the sites. These neighborhood walks lead visitors through specific areas adjacent to the main route of the Literary Trail. Again, each excursion can be taken on its own or as part of a full day of literary touring.

Since many of the sites are privately owned, please respect the properties and their residents. Many sites are open to the public for free or nominal admissions. A list at the end of this book provides complete information on these and other literary landmarks and trails.

Also scattered throughout the text are segments called "Author/ Author!" Though we wanted to include contemporary authors currently living or working in Boston, Cambridge, and Concord, it's likely that few would be pleased to find visitors stopping by their homes. So we asked several of the area's prominent writers to create short pieces about their local inspirations. In prose and poem, they responded with wonderful insights and anecdotes about themselves and about the literary people and places of Greater Boston that had moved their hearts and minds.

WALNUT ST.

Boston
Common

①

②

BEACON ST.

CHARLES ST.

③

Public
Garden

ARLINGTON ST.

⑤   Ⓣ

④

⑥

COMMONWEALTH AVE.

BERKELEY ST.

NEWBURY ST.

BOYLSTON ST.

CLARENDON ST.

Ⓣ

⑦

STORROW DR.

BEACON ST.

DARTMOUTH ST.

⑲

⑱

Ⓣ

⑩

Ⓣ

EXETER ST.

HUNTINGTON AVE.

N

BEACON ST.

MARLBOROUGH ST.

NEWBURY ST.

⑬

COMMONWEALTH AVE.

Ⓣ

MASSACHUSETTS AVE.

⑮

⑯

FENWAY

COMMONWEALTH AVE.

MASSACHUSETTS TURNPIKE

⑭

Ⓣ

BOYLSTON ST.

⑳

1

{BOSTON}

Τ he town of Boston, established by British colonists in 1630, has long been credited as the Cradle of Liberty and the birthplace of the American Revolution.

Less than a century after America's War for Independence, however, the city's image had changed considerably: by then a large, bustling urban center, nineteenth-century Boston became as heralded for its wealth, wit, and wisdom as it had been for its revolutionary roots.

Postcard of Old City Hall, Boston, ca. 1912 (see page 10)

The social and cultural progress of these former Puritans was mani-
fested in a variety of ways. It included social activism, especially in the
areas of abolitionism and women's rights, a religious reawakening and
renewed love of nature that merged into indigenous new philosophies
like transcendentalism, and a literary Golden Age that nurtured many
of the nation's first significant writers, poets, and philosophers as well
as publishing houses, periodicals, bookstores, and libraries.

Two of Boston's most enduring nicknames—"the Athens of
America" and "the Hub of the Solar System"—were direct references
to this Golden Age of the mid-1800s, when the city held a preeminent position in literature and the arts. Athens, after all, had been the
ancient hub of classical culture and learning. Now Boston was laying
its own claim to being the New World's hub—a hive of creativity
around which Nathaniel Hawthorne, Henry Wadsworth Longfellow,
Louisa May Alcott, Harriet Beecher Stowe, Ralph Waldo Emerson,
and other notable literati swarmed like so many illustrious bees.

Turn half-way round, and let your look survey
The white façade that gleams across the way, —
The many-windowed building, tall and wide,
The palace-inn that shows its northern side . . .
Such feasts! The laughs of many a jocund hour
That shook the mortar from King George's tower;
Such guests! What famous names its record boasts,
Whose owners wander in the mob of ghosts!

—OLIVER WENDELL HOLMES, "AT THE SATURDAY CLUB" (1884)

The Boston Literary Trail begins at the **Omni Parker House**, on the corner of School and Tremont streets. Founded in 1855 by a Maine lad named Harvey D. Parker, and renowned as the oldest continuously operating hotel in America, the historic hotel and its restaurants have been credited with a bevy of famous firsts, including the Parker House roll, Boston cream pie (now the official dessert of the state of Massachusetts), and the term *scrod*. It was also known for being the first Boston hotel to offer hot and cold running water in the rooms and the first to import a French chef, who was paid the unprecedented salary of $8,000 a year in the 1850s. Though the elegant old inn has hosted, toasted, or employed numerous celebrities over the decades—from John Wilkes Booth, Charlotte Cushman, Ulysses S. Grant, Sarah Bernhardt, Ho Chi Minh, and Elizabeth Cady Stanton to Joan Crawford, John F. Kennedy, Malcolm X, Babe Ruth, Kelsey Grammer, and Martin Luther King, Jr.—its most famous group of patrons were certainly members of the **Saturday Club**.

Parker House, circa 1860s

Beginning in the mid-1850s, a select group of talented men assembled at the old Parker House (replaced by the current Parker House in 1927) on the last Saturday afternoon of each month. Their notoriously festive roundtables featured readings and intellectual exchanges amid endlessly flowing chatter, mirth, food, and spirits. Though the Saturday Club's members varied over the decades, the early elite included philosopher Ralph Waldo Emerson,

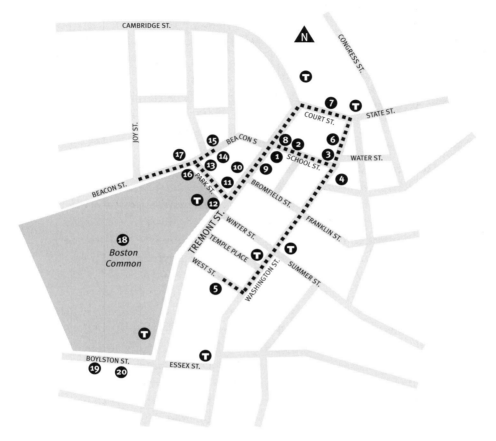

1. Omni Parker House Hotel
2. Site of America's First Public School / Old City Hall
3. Old Corner Bookstore building
4. Old South Meeting House
5. Site of Elizabeth Peabody's Foreign Library and bookstore / Brattle Book Shop
6. Site of Newspaper Row, Pi Alley
7. Site of *New-England Courant* Building
8. King's Chapel Burying Ground
9. Tremont Temple
10. Granary Burying Ground
11. Park Street Church
12. Park Street Station
13. Amory-Ticknor house
14. Boston Athenaeum
15. Former Bellevue Hotel
16. Robert Gould Shaw / 54th Massachusetts Regiment Memorial
17. Massachusetts State House
18. Boston Common
19. Site of Edgar Allan Poe lodgings
20. Colonial Theater

Charles Dickens

poet and *Atlantic Monthly* editor James Russell Lowell, novelist Nathaniel Hawthorne, poets John Greenleaf Whittier and Henry Wadsworth Longfellow, and "autocrat of the breakfast table" Oliver Wendell Holmes.

International literary stars like Britain's **Charles Dickens** (1812–1870) also dropped by for stimulating afternoons with these Parker House patrons. In an 1867 letter to his daughter, Dickens gushed about the marvels of Boston's finest new hotel:

This is an immense hotel, with all manner of white marble public passages and public rooms. I live in a corner, high up, and have a hot and cold bath in my bedroom (connecting with the sitting room) and comforts not in existence when I was here before. The cost of living is enormous, but happily we can afford it. I dine today with Longfellow, Emerson, Holmes, and [Louis] Agassiz. Longfellow was here yesterday. Perfectly white in hair and beard, but a remarkably handsome and notable-looking man.

Dickens's presence in Boston always created a stir. When staying at Parker's, he took lengthy walks most every afternoon, flamboyantly dressed in a brightly colored coat and shiny boots, neatly accessorized with a striped cravat, fine hat, and gloves. Guards were regularly assigned to his hotel room door, since curious fans were eager to watch the novelist rehearsing the exaggerated gestures and odd facial expressions he used to create characters in his animated public readings.

Animation also got Dickens in trouble one festive night, as remembered by Annie Fields in *Memories of a Hostess* (1922):

After the dinner (at the Parker) the other night, Mr. Dickens thought he would take a warm bath; but, the water being drawn, he began playing the clown in pantomime on the edge of the bath (with his clothes on). . . . [I]n a moment, and before he knew where he was, he had tumbled in head over heels, clothes and all.

This wealth of prestigious clients ensured the Parker House a prominent place in literary history: here Dickens gave his first

American reading of "A Christmas Carol" before presenting it to audiences at the nearby Tremont Theater; here Longfellow drafted "Paul Revere's Ride"; and here the idea for the *Atlantic Monthly* was born.

Visitors to the Omni Parker House can still see the fireplace mantel from Dickens's old room and the mirror he used for practicing his performance gestures. You can also enjoy Parker's Bar, where the Saturday Club met, as well as the Press Room, where John F. Kennedy announced his bid for Congress in 1946.

Too far afield to be on the Literary Trail is the **John F. Kennedy Library and Museum**. Opened in 1979 near the campus of the University of Massachusetts at Columbia Point, the library holds many treasures connected with the Bay State's legendary political son, who won the Pulitzer Prize in 1957 for *Profiles in Courage*. A literary bonus is the Kennedy Library's collection of Ernest Hemingway's books, papers, and memorabilia, donated by his widow, Mary Hemingway. A second place to discover roots of the Kennedy legacy is the former president's birthplace and childhood home, now the **John F. Kennedy National Historic Site**, located at 83 Beals Street in the neighboring town of Brookline.

Another significant site that's connected to Parker House personnel but many miles off the trail is the home of **Malcolm X** (1925–1965), at 72 Dale Street, Roxbury. Born in Omaha, Nebraska, Malcolm Little spent his formative years in Boston. In the period immediately preceding America's entrance into World War II, teenage Malcolm was a busboy at the Parker House. Scarred by a difficult childhood — his father was murdered and his mother institutionalized—Malcolm quickly entered a life of crime, ending up in the Charlestown (Massachusetts) State Prison. Here he discovered the Black Muslim faith, which changed his life.

Malcolm X

In *The Autobiography of Malcolm X* (1965), coauthored with Alex Haley, the radical black leader credited the Hub with his conversion and salvation: "All praise is due to Allah that I moved to Boston when I did. If I hadn't, I'd probably still be a brain-washed black Christian."

Across from the School Street entrance to the Omni Parker House, embedded in the sidewalk, is a folk art mosaic by Lilli Ann Killen Rosenberg. This spot, lodged behind the rough granite exterior of King's Chapel, was the original site of **America's first public school**, the precursor of the Boston Latin School. Among its early alumni were Ralph Waldo Emerson, Cotton Mather, Edward Everett Hale, John Hancock, Samuel Adams, William Ellery Channing, Henry Ward Beecher, Francis Parkman, and James Freeman Clarke. Its most famous dropout was Benjamin Franklin.

Though he left the school, the versatile Franklin is still hovering nearby. In the courtyard behind the Latin School site, a larger-than-life bronze statue of a mature Franklin shares the space with Josiah Quincy. When Richard Saltonstall Greenough was sculpting the realistic image, he copied one of Franklin's fur-trimmed suits, now owned by the Massachusetts Historical Society. The 1856 sculpture was the first public portrait statue erected in Boston. Author and lawyer Josiah Quincy—whose statue was crafted by Thomas Ball in 1879—was a president of Harvard College and one of three Josiah Quincys to serve as mayor of Boston during the nineteenth century.

The large wedding cake–like structure looming over Franklin, Quincy, and the courtyard is **Old City Hall** (see image on page 4), whose most colorful occupant was yet another Boston mayor, **James Michael Curley** (1874–1958), the heroic and controversial "Mayor of the Poor" who dominated Boston politics for the first half of the twentieth century. Both the structure and the mayor were commemorated in *The Last Hurrah* (1956). Its author, **Edwin O'Connor** (1918–1968), began his professional career as a radio announcer and producer, and a reviewer for the *Boston Herald*. Still, his fiction is the stuff for which he will always be remembered. (His 1961 novel *The Edge of Sadness* was awarded the Pulitzer Prize.)

Though O'Connor denied the connection, he clearly modeled *The Last Hurrah*'s Frank Skeffington, Jr., after Curley and his city hall after what he called this "lunatic pile of a building: a great, grim, resolutely

I'm not just an elected official of the city;
I'm a tribal chieftain as well.

—FRANK SKEFFINGTON, JR., IN *THE LAST HURRAH* (1956)

Last Hurrah movie still with
Spencer Tracy, 1958

ugly dust-catcher." In a chance meeting with O'Connor outside the Parker House in 1956, Curley thanked the author for his novel, adding that he especially liked "the part where I die." Surprised by the popularity of *The Last Hurrah*, Curley even rode the wave by writing his own autobiography, *I'd Do It Again* (1957).

While working at Old City Hall or at the State House up the street, Curley—a roguish Irish-American politician of limited morality and unlimited charm—held power lunches and tipped silver dollars in the main dining room of the Parker House. It's no coincidence that since 1969, "The Last Hurrah" has been the name of one of the Omni Parker House's popular bars.

Curley's life and character have intrigued many writers and inspired many books, from Joseph Dineen's *The Purple Shamrock* (1949) to James Carroll's *Mortal Friends* (1978) and Jack Beatty's *The Rascal King* (1992).

Follow School Street down to the intersection with Washington, where one of Boston's most curious structures—the building that once housed the **Old Corner Bookstore**—still stands. Built in 1718 as a home and apothecary shop by Dr. Thomas Crease, it served that dual purpose for a series of pharmacists and physicians for more than a hundred years. In the nineteenth century, however, it became an internationally known literary center—the simple site where, between 1845 and 1865, **William D. Ticknor** (1810–1864) and **James T. Fields** (1817–1881) revolutionized the world of American book publishing.

Old Corner Bookstore

Beginning in 1829, Carter & Hendee, then Ticknor & Allen, became the first of ten firms of booksellers and publishers to be housed here over the next seventy-five years. By 1837, young William Ticknor was running the show, assisted by a bright, witty, versatile, and ambitious apprentice named James T. ("Jamie") Fields.

Before promoting Fields, then making him a partner, Ticknor ran a solid, nondescript shop that occasionally published books—usually at the authors' expense. Once Fields shared the helm, the Old Corner Bookstore was on the road to worldwide renown as a well-stocked shop, a prominent publishing house, and a magnet for the literary world.

To lure authors and secure exclusive publishing rights in the United States, Fields devised the nation's first system of royalties. He also arranged ownership of prestigious magazines like the *North American Review* and the fledgling *Atlantic Monthly,* in which his writers regularly appeared.

A sincere friend, guardian, and literary counselor to his flock of writers, Fields was also an entrepreneurial huckster with a flair for promotion. He organized and publicized speaking tours—including Dickens's lucrative lecture circuit of 1867–1868—and was not above "buying" reviewers, inventing facts about his authors, planting publicity in periodicals, and writing glowing reviews of his own books under fabricated names.

In *From the Easy Chair* (1892–1894), George William Curtis beautifully described the allure of Fields and the Old Corner:

> *The annals of publishing and the traditions of publishers in this country will always mention the little Corner Bookstore in Boston . . . , and those who recall it in other days will always remember the curtained desk at which poet and philosopher and historian and divine, and the doubting,*

I never can go into that famous Corner Bookstore and look over the new books in the row before me, as I enter the door, without seeing half a dozen which I want to read or at least know about. The titles of many of them interest me. I look into one or two, perhaps. I have sometimes picked up a line of a sentence, in those momentary glances through the uncut leaves of a new book, which I have never forgotten.

—OLIVER WENDELL HOLMES

timid young author, were sure to see the bright face and to hear the hearty welcome of James T. Fields. What a crowded, busy shop it was, with the shelves full of books, and piles of books upon the counters and tables. . . .

[Here, at the Old Corner Bookstore, was] the Exchange of Wit, the Rialto of current good things, the hub of the Hub. . . . It was a very remarkable group of men — indeed, it was the first group of really great American authors—which familiarly frequented the corner as guests of [Jamie] Fields. . . . It was that circle which compelled the world to acknowledge that there was an American literature. Of most of these authors the house at the corner came to be the publishers, and to the end they maintained the warmest relations with Fields, who was not their publisher only, but their appreciative and sympathetic friend.

Among the dozens of prominent writers who worked with Ticknor & Fields—and who passed through the store's portals with startling regularity—were Harriet Beecher Stowe and Henry David Thoreau, as well as Emerson, Longfellow, Holmes, Whittier, and Dickens. If Boston was "the Hub of the Solar System," the Old Corner Bookstore was surely "the Hub of the Hub," as acknowledged in this comment from *Harper's Magazine:* "The Old Corner is so popular a resort that all Boston, with little exaggeration, may be said to pass through it in a day."

James T. Fields had a special talent for uncovering, encouraging, and publishing gems by local writers. One of his favorite stories, as recounted in *Yesterdays with Authors* (1871), was pulling a particular manuscript from the reclusive Nathaniel Hawthorne. True or not—and there is a question about its authenticity—it's nevertheless a fine tale:

I was hurrying down the stairs when [Hawthorne] called after me from the chamber, asking me to stop a moment. Then quickly stepping into the entry with a roll of manuscript in his hands, he said: "How in Heaven's name did you know this thing was there? As you have found me out, take what I have written, and tell me, after you get home and have time to read it, if it is good for anything. It is either very good or very bad,—I don't know which."

James T. Fields, Nathaniel
Hawthorne, and George Ticknor

*On my way up to Boston I read the germ of "*The Scarlet Letter.*"...*

Fields, of course, had his literary misses as well. When a teacher named Louisa May Alcott brought him some recent work, he responded, "Stick to your teaching; you can't write." He then loaned the young Alcott forty dollars for classroom books and chairs, saying she could return the cash if and when she made her fortune.

Three years after the roaring success of *Little Women* (1868), Alcott sent Fields the cash, along with a brief, bemused note:

Dear Mr. Fields
Once upon a time you lent me forty dollars, kindly saying I might return them when I had made 'a pot of gold.'
As the miracle has been unexpectedly wrought I wish to fulfil my part of the bargain, & herewith repay my debt with many thanks.
Very truly yours
L. M. ALCOTT

The publishing company Houghton Mifflin, still in Boston, is a direct descendant of Ticknor & Fields. In 1979, Houghton restored the Ticknor & Fields imprint as a tribute to its predecessor.

James T. Fields's first wife, Eliza Josephine Willard, died a few months after their marriage in 1850. Four years later, Fields married Eliza's nineteen-year-old cousin, Annie Adams.

As it turned out, **Annie Adams Fields** (1834–1915) became a cultural icon herself, holding court and hosting salons for her literary, theatrical, and artistic friends in her home at 148 (originally 37) Charles Street. Her guests included many of the Ticknor & Fields and Saturday Club regulars, as well as **Sarah Orne Jewett** (1849–1909)— Annie's companion for many years in a "Boston marriage"—and their protégée, Willa Cather. Other literary women supported by Annie Fields included poet Louise Imogen Guiney and author Harriet Beecher Stowe.

Annie Adams Fields, watercolor on ivory by Lucia Fairchild Fuller, based on an 1855 daguerrotype

Oliver Wendell Holmes, in an 1881 Christmas letter to Annie Fields, recalled the galaxy of talent that congregated in her Charles Street home:

Under your roof I have met more visitors to be remembered than under any other. But for your hospitality I should never have had the privilege of personal acquaintance with famous writers and artists whom I can now recall as I saw them, talked with them, heard them in that pleasant library, that most lively and agreeable dining-room.

The site of the Old Corner Bookstore, incidentally, has literary connections that predate Ticknor & Fields by two centuries. In 1634, only four years after English settlers arrived in the area, **Anne Hutchinson** and her husband built a home on this corner. Hutchinson was a popular, prominent midwife and brilliant thinker who challenged the all-male Puritan hierarchy on their strict and exclusive religious and social viewpoints. A variety of similarly rebellious women—including Quaker **Mary Dyer**—met regularly for discussion groups and prayer at Hutchinson's home, soon threatening the Puritan status quo and ultimately dooming Hutchinson to banishment. Colonial Boston was clearly not ready to embrace her quest for freedom of speech and thought.

Other prominent neighbors from this early colonial period were **Governor John Winthrop**, whose journals chronicled the early history of Boston, and the **Reverend Cotton Mather** (ca. 1663–1728), whose numerous sermons were an essential element in colonial literature.

The Reverend Mather was one of many literary Mathers in the New World, beginning with his grandfather Richard (1596–1669), a contributor to the 1640 *Bay Psalm Book*. Cotton Mather himself, a Harvard graduate, had more than 2,000 volumes in his library. He also wrote 444 books of his own, including *The Wonders of the Invisible World* and the 1,300-page *Magnalia Christi Americana*, about the Salem witch trials. The powerful, persuasive Mather was hated by many, including the twentieth-century poet Robert Lowell, who observed that "the Salem witch-hanger was a professional man of letters employed to moralize and subdue."

Though the Old Corner Bookstore is an important landmark today, it was not always so. In 1903, four decades after the departure of Ticknor & Fields, the last of the series of booksellers left, and the building went through a number of incarnations, from haberdashery to photo supply store. By 1960, the nearly unrecognizable, deteriorated structure housed a pizza parlor and was plastered with outdoor billboards. Moreover, developers interested in urban renewal were eyeing the site as a prime spot for a parking lot.

The threat of demolition inspired a group of Bostonians—including the Athenaeum's director, Walter Muir Whitehill, and John Codman, chairman of the Beacon Hill Architectural Commission—to organize a nonprofit organization, Historic Boston Incorporated. With encouragement from the City of Boston, private donations from around the country, and a bank loan (which the *Boston Globe* later helped them repay), HBI took title to the building at the end of 1960. For the next

The Reverend Cotton Mather

twenty-five years, the historic exterior was restored and the interior modernized for retail and office spaces; beginning in the late 1990s, the building became the subject of a historic structures report and embarked on an even more historically accurate restoration. Meanwhile, modern uses of the interior have included bookstores, *Boston Globe* offices, and headquarters for Historic Boston Incorporated, the Freedom Trail Foundation, and the Boston Adult Literacy Fund.

Diagonally across from the Old Corner Bookstore, at 310 Washington Street, is the **Old South Meeting House**, a pivotal meeting place for patriots at the onset of the American Revolution. Now a beautifully renovated and active cultural center and museum, the Old South once had a congregation that included two eighteenth-century literary lights: Phillis Wheatley, America's first published black poet, and Benjamin Franklin, who was born a stone's throw away. Franklin wrote his first prose while working nearby, at his brother's print shop on Court Street.

In the 1870s, the Old South was threatened with demolition. Philanthropist Mary Hemenway led the effort to save it, engaging some of Boston's most eminent citizens—like Julia Ward Howe, Ralph Waldo Emerson, Louisa May Alcott, James Russell Lowell, and Wendell Phillips—to do public readings from their works here and to plea for the building's salvation. Historian and author Walter Muir Whitehill later praised America's first successful urban historic preservation venture, noting that saving the Old South was "the first instance in Boston where respect for the historical and architectural heritage of the city triumphed over considerations of profit, expediency, laziness, and vulgar convenience."

Fiery orators, incidentally, have held forth at the Old South since it first opened its doors in 1729. During the building's first 143 years, ministers and political pundits held sway; since then, the impressive roster of speakers has included twenty-first-century figures such as Al Gore, Howard Zinn, Coretta Scott King, and David McCullough. The Old South has long hosted two lecture series: Middays at the Meeting House and the prestigious Ford Hall Forum, the nation's oldest free public lecture series.

If you are on foot, you can take a side trip here. With the Old South on your left and the Old Corner behind you, follow

Washington Street to the busy shopping district called Downtown Crossing. Four blocks from School Street, at 13–15 West Street, is a plaque marking the site of Elizabeth Peabody's **Foreign Library and bookstore**.

Elizabeth Palmer Peabody (1804–1894) was a transcendentalist who founded America's first kindergartens and became Boston's first female publisher. The store she ran at the front of her home on West Street became a vibrant literary gathering place, in part because she stocked many foreign books and periodicals. In the parlor behind the bookshop, Elizabeth's sister Mary married innovative educator Horace Mann and her sister Sophia married author Nathaniel Hawthorne.

Mary Peabody (1806–1887) was an author in her own right, seeking to improve humanity with such volumes as *The Flower People and Christianity in the Kitchen: A Physiological Cookbook*. **Sophia Peabody** (1809–1871) was a reclusive painter who fell in love with the equally reclusive and extremely handsome Hawthorne, creating what contemporary author Shaun O'Connell called "one of the few happy marriages in American literary history."

The *grande dame* **Elizabeth Peabody**, who lived to the age of ninety, was a veritable legend in her own time—a moral teacher, educational reformer, abolitionist, feminist, biographer, publisher, and patron of the arts. She supported the literary world tirelessly, joining Bronson Alcott's radical Temple School in 1834, helping Nathaniel Hawthorne secure a job at the Custom House, publishing Thoreau's essay "Civil Disobedience," paying for the publication of the transcendentalist journal the *Dial*, and inspiring those around her to reason, write, and create.

Though he flatly denied it, Henry James clearly used Elizabeth Peabody as a model for Miss Birdseye in *The Bostonians* (1886). Early in that novel, feminist Olive Chancellor describes Birdseye—an ardent transcendentalist and devotee of Emerson—to a handsome southern intruder, Basil Ransom:

Elizabeth Peabody

"And who is Miss Birdseye?"

"She is one of our celebrities. She is the woman in the world, I suppose, who has laboured most for every wise reform. I think I ought to tell you," Miss Chancellor went on in a moment, "she was one of the earliest, one of the most passionate, of the old Abolitionists."

She had thought, indeed, she ought to tell him that, and it threw her into a little tremor of excitement to do so. Yet, if she had been afraid he would show some irritation at this news, she was disappointed at the geniality with which he exclaimed:

"Why, poor old lady—she must be quite mature!"

The most important literary events at Elizabeth Peabody's bookstore, however, were undoubtedly the "Conversations" held between 1839 and 1844 by the brilliant and intense **Margaret Fuller** (1810–1850). For five years, Wednesday afternoons at 15 West Street were devoted to stimulating discussions on topics as diverse as art, education, ethics, health, mythology, heroes, and women's rights. The women—and later, the men as well—Fuller attracted to her "Conversations" were a *Who's Who* of progressive Boston in the 1840s. As Fuller later explained:

[M]en are called on from an early period to reproduce all that they learn. Their college exercises, their political duties, their professional studies . . . call on them to put to use what they have learned. But women learn without any attempt to reproduce. Their only reproduction is for purposes of display. It is to supply this defect that these conversations have been planned.

One significant outgrowth of these meetings was Fuller's magnum

Margaret Fuller

opus, *Woman in the Nineteenth Century* (1845), a groundbreaking exploration of early feminism.

Born in Cambridgeport in 1810 and raised by a stern father who would have preferred a boy, Margaret Fuller was rewarded with a boy's education: she was reading Ovid, Virgil, and Horace by the age of eight and was immersed in classical literature throughout her teen years; she was also the first woman to be allowed to use the Harvard College Library. In time, Fuller became a respected critic and pioneering female reporter for the *New York Tribune*. Having the brilliant "mind of a man"—not to mention a large-boned body and mannerisms that many considered masculine—Fuller was an intimidating presence. Equally disconcerting was her unwillingness to hide these strengths, as evidenced in this comment from *Memoirs of Margaret Fuller Ossoli* (1852): "I now know all the people worth knowing in America, and I find no intellect comparable to my own."

Many of America's most respected thinkers—such as Bronson Alcott and Ralph Waldo Emerson—were clearly taken with Fuller's personal magnetism, and accepted her as an intellectual equal. Alcott hired her to teach languages at his progressive Temple School. As a member of Emerson's Hedges Club, Fuller helped the philosopher develop the concept of transcendentalism; as an editor of the *Dial*, she and Emerson sustained a national showcase for essays by the cream of the transcendentalist crop. Julia Ward Howe, in her 1883 biography of Fuller, noted the differences between these two brilliant colleagues and friends:

> *While Mr. Emerson never appeared to be modified by any change of circumstance, never melted nor took fire, but was always and everywhere himself, the soul of Margaret was subject to a glowing passion which raised the temperature of the social atmosphere around her.*

Fuller's promising future was cut short in 1850, in her fortieth year. Returning home from Italy—where she covered the Italian revolutions and secretly married Marquis Angelo Ossoli—her ship ran aground off Fire Island, New York. Fuller, Ossoli, and their infant son all drowned. A distraught Emerson sent Thoreau to survey the wreckage, but no remnants of Fuller or Ossoli were ever found.

Fuller's dynamic persona lived on in memory and literature. It's likely, for example, that she provided the inspiration for many literary characters, including Zenobia in Hawthorne's *The Blithedale Romance* (1852) and Miranda in James Russell Lowell's *A Fable for Critics* (1848).

Before leaving this area, stop by the venerable **Brattle Book Shop** at 9 West Street. Founded in 1825 (and originally located on nearby Brattle Street), the store was in business when Peabody, Fuller, and others held forth during Boston's literary Golden Age. One of the oldest and largest antiquarian bookstores in the country, it's still a fine place to spend an afternoon browsing for treasures.

Retrace your path along Washington Street. One block before School Street you'll see Bromfield Street on your left and Franklin Street on your right. **The Studio Building**, at the corner of Bromfield and Tremont, was originally the working space for many artists. Daniel Chester French—a sculptor linked to Boston's literary history, who appears throughout the Literary Trail—once shared studio space here.

Three blocks down Franklin Street, at the corner of Federal, is the site of the **Federal Street** (also known as **Boston**) **Theater**. Opened in 1794 as Boston's first legitimate theater, the Federal enjoyed several decades of performances until it closed in 1852.

Among the writers whose plays were produced here was **Susanna Haswell Rowson** (1762-1824), an English educator, school administrator, actor, lecturer, playwright, poet, and novelist who made her home in Boston. Rowson is best known for her morality tale for young women, *Charlotte Temple* (1791), which remained America's best-selling novel until 1852, when Harriet Beecher Stowe's *Uncle Tom's Cabin* took its place.

A contemporary of Rowson's was **Judith Sargent Murray** (1751–1820), whose satirical works for the stage, *The Medium or Happy Tea Party* and *The Traveller Returned*, were produced at the Federal Street Theater in 1795 and 1796. Murray was well respected as a poet for a variety of Boston journals and a regular columnist for the *Massachusetts Magazine*, where, under a male pseudonym, she discussed women's equality, politics, and education. When these columns were collected in her book, *The Gleaner* (1798), Murray became the first American woman to publish her own work.

Return to the corner of Washington and School streets, by the new Irish Famine Memorial (1998). The literary tradition lives on in this

Newspaper Row, 1889   Postcard of Pi Alley, circa 1910

historic area of Boston, with bookstores offering ample volumes on the city's social and political heritage. Not far from here are several other sites important in America's literary history.

From the nineteenth through the middle of the twentieth century, the area around Washington, Court, and State streets was known as **Newspaper Row**. This strip was once the home of many of Boston's most powerful newspapers—including the *Boston Globe*, the *Transcript*, the *Herald*, the *Post*, the *Traveler*, and the *Journal*—and was renowned as "the Cradle of American Journalism." Off Washington Street is the long alcove known as **Pi Alley**, so named for the small jumbles of press type, called "pi," often strewn about here.

Though modern Bostonians have grown used to seeing two daily newspapers, the *Boston Globe* and the *Boston Herald*, their forebears were offered many more newspapers, and many more editions. In *The Proper Bostonians* (1947), Cleveland Amory mused on the heyday of the old *Transcript*, the Hub's society rag, whose offices stood at the corner of Milk and Washington streets:

> *It is doubtful if Boston's institution men would ever have achieved such prominence in their city if they had not had a voice to carry their "way of life" to the Proper Bostonian masses. They found this voice in one of the all-time curiosities of American journalism, the Boston* Evening Transcript. . . . *Not to read the* Transcript *was unthinkable. It was*

never a newspaper in the vulgar sense of the word. The story of three rep-
resentatives of the press who were received into a Beacon Hill home
with a servant's announcement, "Two reporters from the papers, Sir, and
a gentleman from the Transcript," *was actually a legend once removed*
from the London Times, *but it became the Boston paper's trademark.*
The loyalty of its readers was proverbial. In the wind of its editorial
opinion they swayed, said the poet T. S. Eliot, "like a field of ripe corn."

This section of Washington Street, Boston's oldest thoroughfare, was originally called Cornhill. Even in colonial and early federal times, it was a bustling center of book publishing and sales. **Edgar Allan Poe**'s first book, *Tamerlane and Other Poems*, was published anonymously in 1827 in a building at the corner of Washington and State (formerly King) streets.

At the corner of King and Kirby streets was the home of the successful tailor and merchant John Wheatley and his wife, Susanna. When a frail, sickly child of seven or eight arrived in Boston in 1761 on a slave ship from West Africa, the Wheatleys purchased her as a household servant. The family called the girl "Phillis" after the slave ship, and—as was the custom—gave her their own last name.

Under the tutelage of Susanna and her teenage twins, Nathaniel and Mary, **Phillis Wheatley** (ca. 1753–1784) learned to speak, read, and write English in only sixteen months. She also studied Latin, geography, history, the classics, and the Bible, and she was actively writing poetry by the age of twelve. Her first poem was "On the Reverend Joseph Sewall When Sick," about the pastor of the Old South Meeting House, whose congregation she joined in 1771.

Poetry eventually brought Phillis international fame. When

Phillis Wheatley

I, young in life, by seeming cruel fate
Was snatch'd from Afric's fancy'd happy seat:
What pangs excruciating must molest,
What sorrows labour in my parents breast?

—PHILLIS WHEATLEY, "LETTER TO EARL OF DARTMOUTH" (1772)

---

her first book—*Poems on Various Subjects, Religious and Moral* (1773)—was rejected by a Boston printer, she published it with bookseller-publisher Archibald Bell in London, supported by Selina Hastings, the countess of Huntington. And when some expressed doubt that a slave could have written such excellent verse, Phillis submitted to an interrogation by a panel of men—including seven ministers, Governor Thomas Hutchinson, and John Hancock—and passed with the highest praise.

Though many have criticized the quality of Wheatley's verse, her style reflected the popular tastes of the day and included many elegies and tributes to God or great men, with themes of learning, virtue, and redemption through Christ. One such poem, dedicated to General George Washington of the Continental Army, earned her warm thanks and an invitation to Washington's headquarters in Cambridge. That house is now known for a later owner, who lived there far longer than General Washington—Henry Wadsworth Longfellow.

At the intersection of Washington, State, and Court streets, you are facing the Old State House and the downtown Visitor Center for Boston National Historical Park.

Though not a part of the Literary Trail, the Old State House and Faneuil Hall—two blocks farther down Congress Street—are both significant stops on the Revolutionary Freedom Trail and landmarks of free speech in America.

At the Old State House, colonial patriot and lawyer James Otis argued against the Writs of Assistance, paving the way for the American Revolution. Here the Declaration of Independence was first read aloud to the town of Boston in 1776, and here abolitionist William Lloyd Garrison hid in 1835, when an angry mob tried to lynch him for his views. The Bostonian Society, which operates a stellar library of Boston history across the way, has run the Old State House as a museum since 1882.

Patricia Smith on Phillis Wheatley

A blade edge glints from the vowels
of such simple words, written in
nervous, new girl cursive—there were
never chains to escape from, only
her own skin, black prison, sweet cage.
She endured the pale, well-meaning hands
patting her head, resting on the tamed naps
of her hair, she smiled while men cooed
in awed praise of those slices from her soul,
those rhythm shrieks, those prayers out loud
set down in neat couplets, line after chopped line
of words she wasn't supposed to know.
Such a good girl, so smart, well-spoken,
crisp blouse buttoned tight at her throat,
writing words right enough to sing, almost
like she was
free.

She wrote of freedom so deftly, there seemed
to be no reason she couldn't rise from her desk
and walk into the shelter of a million waiting arms,
no reason she couldn't open her mouth wide,
throw back her head, pop loose imprisoned hips
and dance until the pink bottoms of her feet
were threaded with soul. There were never
real chains to escape from, only this dream
she kept having, the feel of a million white hands
resting proudly on her head. Each time she
wrote of freedom, tasted its potent mix
of iron and sunlight, she remembered Boston.

America's first face, breathing outside her window.
Boston was a skewered rhyme, books with
gilt-edged pages, the flat smack of a whip
on the flanks of a tired horse. Boston was
her teacher, her captor, her crotchety muse,
taunting her with the promise of free,
a wild someday dance on weary feet.
She was lucky. Boston was the perfect place
to settle behind a desk of scarred wood,
light a candle, dip an old pen into pitch-black ink,
touch that pen to paper, and begin to scream again.

To reach Faneuil Hall, take a right turn down State Street past the Old State House, then a left on Congress Street.

Faneuil Hall, opened in 1742 and enlarged by Charles Bulfinch in 1805, was called "the Cradle of Liberty"—a term later applied to all of Boston. From its stage Samuel Adams advocated the overthrow of British rule, William Lloyd Garrison appealed for an end to slavery, Susan B. Anthony denounced the inferior status of women, and John F. Kennedy gave his final speech before winning the presidency in 1960.

The ground-level shops under Faneuil Hall and the numerous Faneuil Hall Marketplace stores nearby are a shopper's and food lover's paradise, with several well-stocked bookstores to boot.

Benjamin Franklin

Return to the Old State House, at the junction of Court and Washington streets. As you go up Court Street, you'll pass on the right a plaque marking the site of the *New-England Courant*, one of Boston's earliest newspapers. When James Franklin began the *Courant* in 1721, he created the fourth newspaper ever printed in the British colonies. More important, he quickly attracted some of the quickest, cleverest, and most rebellious writers around—including his kid brother Ben.

Benjamin Franklin (1706–1790), the fifteenth of seventeen Franklin children, was not hired as a writer. At the age of twelve, Ben began an arduous, often cruel and exploitative nine-year apprenticeship to brother James. Despite only two years of formal education, Ben was bright, well read, and self-confident. Between his menial duties at the newspaper, he read from James's ample library, absorbed the insights of the *Courant*'s writers, learned Boston inside and out, and mastered the skills of editing, printing, and distributing a newspaper.

Unbeknownst to his brother, Ben also became a popular columnist. For six months in 1722, Ben secretly composed and submitted to the paper a series of fourteen witty, often wise and biting essays on topics from virginity, hoop petticoats, and insincere funeral elegies to the quality of education at Harvard and the cultural life of the Commonwealth. Under the whimsical moniker of Silence Dogood— the imaginary widow of a Harvard minister—Ben also touched on women's liberation and the poverty of widowhood. Slipped under James's door at night, the columns had an impact on Boston's social and political life—not to mention its gossip.

The ruse didn't last. Nor did Ben's willingness to complete his apprenticeship in the repressive Puritan town of Boston. At seventeen, he moved to New York, then Philadelphia, and became the philosopher, essayist, newspaperman, diplomat, politician, scientist, and inventor we recall today.

The first edition of *The Autobiography of Benjamin Franklin* was published in France in 1791, one year after Franklin's death. The first English edition appeared in 1793, and became one of the most popular books ever printed in the English-speaking world. Since then, the *Autobiography* has been translated into dozens of languages and editions—and has never been out of print.

Follow Court Street up to Tremont Street, bearing left on Tremont to the **King's Chapel Burying Ground**, Boston's oldest graveyard. Nathaniel Hawthorne visited here when he worked at the Custom House or did research at the Boston Athenaeum. James T. Fields, in *Yesterdays with Authors* (1871), recalled Hawthorne's affinity for burying grounds: "He very rarely described himself as inside a church, but he liked to wander among the graves in the churchyards and read the epitaphs on the moss-grown slabs."

Since the 1920s, the legend has grown that the gravestone of Elizabeth Pain (d. 1704) inspired the character of Hester Prynne in Hawthorne's great novel *The Scarlet Letter* (1850). Though the connection is unsubstantiated and unlikely, the heraldic symbol on Pain's grave, on the path nearest the side wall of King's Chapel, can be vaguely seen to resemble a stylized "A." Inspired by Pain's headstone or not, the vision of Hester Prynne's grave provided Hawthorne with a chilling finish to his novel:

And, after many, many years, a new grave was delved, near an old and sunken one, in that burial-ground beside which King's Chapel has since been built. . . . All around there were monuments carved with armorial bearings; and on this simple slab of slate . . . there appeared the semblance of an engraved escutcheon . . . "ON A FIELD, SABLE, THE LETTER A, GULES."

Though **King's Chapel** borders King's Chapel Burying Ground, the two sites are totally unrelated. The Puritan graveyard dates from 1630, while the rustic stone chapel next door was built more than a century later by Anglicans—the church that Puritans had deliberately fled from when coming to America. King's Chapel served as the first Anglican church in New England and later, the first Unitarian Church in America. That curious history explains, in part, the church's unique formal liturgy and its use of an unusual volume in its services, the *Book of Common Prayer According to the Use in King's Chapel.*

When A. Bronson Alcott and Abigail May decided to formally commit their lives to one another in 1830, they chose King's Chapel and one Reverend Mr. Greenwood for their wedding ceremony. Though Bronson and Abigail were well known in their own right, it was their daughter, Louisa May Alcott of *Little Women* fame, who eventually brought them everlasting renown.

Continue down Tremont Street, past the Omni Parker House on your left. Stop for a moment by **Tremont Temple**, an active Baptist church whose roots go back to the early nineteenth century. The original structure was the old Tremont Theater, which opened in 1827. By 1840, however, Boston's theaters were besieged by religious revivalists who considered public stages bastions of immorality. Hence, in 1843, the structure was sold to a new Baptist congregation, which espoused the radical concept that blacks and whites could worship together in complete equality. What was called the First Baptist Free Church became the first truly integrated church in America.

Though the building (in four different incarnations) has been a house of worship ever since, it never abandoned the theatrical world. Even during its first decade, Tremont Temple was continually leased to producers of plays and musical events as well as to political orators and writers.

Abraham Lincoln spoke here, as did every American president thereafter through Herbert Hoover. Daniel Webster waxed eloquent from the boards of Tremont Temple, as did Edward Everett, William Lloyd Garrison, Frederick Douglass, Eugene Debs, Helen Keller, the Reverend Billy Sunday, the Reverend Billy Graham, and a host of others. Sitting in the audience, Harriet Beecher Stowe was given a standing ovation when the Emancipation Proclamation was first read aloud here in 1863. And when Charles Dickens gave theatrical readings during his 1867–1868 American tour, he packed the house at Tremont Temple every night.

During one of Will Rogers's visits to Boston in 1930, he attended a service at Tremont Temple Baptist Church. Asked by the press to say a few words, Rogers quipped, "When I die, my epitaph . . . is going to read, 'I joked about every prominent man of my time, but I never met a man I didn't like.' I am proud of that. I can hardly wait to die so it can be carved."

The remark was connected to the humorist forever after.

Farther down Tremont is the legendary **Granary Burying Ground**, the permanent home of many heroes of the American Revolution, including firebrand Samuel Adams, revolutionary bankroller John Hancock, impassioned orator James Otis, the five victims of the Boston Massacre, and midnight rider Paul Revere. The family of Benjamin Franklin—though not Ben himself—is also buried here.

An interesting gentleman interred at the Granary, who predates the revolutionary crowd by a century, is **Samuel Sewall** (1652–1730). Born in England and educated to the ministry at Harvard, Sewall became best known as one of the judges who tried the Salem witchcraft cases of 1692. He was the *only* member of his Puritan peer group who publicly apologized for the nineteen convictions that resulted, accepting "blame and shame" for his actions. Sewall's most famous literary work was a three-volume *Diary*, an acclaimed record of fascinating minutiae about life, thought, politics, religion, culture, business, fashion, and weather in colonial Boston. Written between 1673 and 1729, the diary was published by the Massachusetts Historical Society in 1878–1882. Equally important was Sewall's work *The Selling of Joseph* (1700), credited as the first Puritan antislavery tract in the colonies.

The Granary's most curious link to Boston literary history, however, is the alleged gravesite of "Mother Goose." Boston's **Mother Goose** was **Elizabeth Foster** (1665–1757), the second wife of Isaac Goose or "Vergoose," or perhaps even "Vertigoose." According to one version of the tale, Elizabeth fed, raised, and told stories to sixteen Goose children—six of her own and ten by Isaac's first wife. Another version suggests that she told her grandchildren these stories during her years as a widow. Whatever the timing and audience, the tales she spun were supposedly collected and published in 1719 by her son-in-law Thomas Fleet as *Songs for the Nursery or Mother Goose's Melodies for Children.*

Though the legend endures, it's not likely that Mother Goose is spending eternity at the Granary. One problem is, she has no headstone. Isaac is here, as is his first wife, Mary. But no marker suggests that Elizabeth is by their side. Second, there is no copy extant of Fleet's volume. Moreover, both France and England claim to have nurtured the real Mother Goose—and most of the rhymes we know today can be traced to European origins.

Sarah Josepha Buell Hale

One of America's most popular nursery rhymes did, however, originate with a Boston woman. A patriotic widow named **Sarah Josepha Buell Hale** (1788–1879) organized a glorified bake sale in 1830 to finance the completion of the Bunker Hill Monument; she also helped convince Abraham Lincoln to declare Thanksgiving a national holiday in 1863.

Though she wrote and published poems, short stories, plays, novels, and a women's encyclopedia, Hale is best known as one of America's first female editors. She edited and published the *American Ladies Magazine* (1828–1837) in Boston before moving to Philadelphia to run the popular *Godey's Lady's Book* (1837–1877). Though the latter often featured mediocre writing and sentimental fluff, it also included contributions from Emerson, Longfellow, Stowe, Poe, and Hawthorne.

Hale's most enduring work was a famous nursery rhyme, first published in *Poems for Our Children* (1830) as "Mary's Lamb":

Mary had a little lamb,
Its fleece was white as snow,
And everywhere that Mary went,
That lamb was sure to go.

Some historians, incidentally, doubt Hale's authorship of the poem, and claim she merely published another writer's lines, which she then credited to herself.

Just beyond the Granary, at the corner of Tremont and Park streets, is the **Park Street Church**, which Henry James once called "the most interesting mass of bricks and mortar" in the country. Two important events occurred here on the Fourth of July. In 1829, William Lloyd Garrison gave his first public antislavery address, and in 1831, the song "America" was first sung from the steps of the church. Popularly known as "My Country 'Tis of Thee," the lyrics were written by the young Samuel Francis Smith of Boston, who was then preparing for the ministry at Andover Theological Seminary.

Across the street is the **Park Street Station** of the Massachusetts Bay Transportation Authority (MBTA). Opened in 1897, this station was one of the four original stops on America's first subway system. The beloved old station and its subway have been heralded in sonnet and song over the past century: Oliver Wendell Holmes waxed poetic about it in "The Broomstick Train," A. J. Deutsch wrote an eerie science fiction tale about a train bound for Cambridge in "A Subway Named Mobius" (1950), and the Kingston Trio had a smash hit, "M.T.A.," in 1959 with their song about poor Charlie, who couldn't pay the new five-cent exit fare:

Charlie's wife goes down to the Scollay Square Station
Every day at quarter past two,
And through the open window she hands Charlie a sandwich
As the train comes rumblin' through.

Did he ever return? No, he never returned,
And his fate is still unlearned.
He may ride forever through the streets of Boston,
He's the man who never returned.

Incidentally, "M.T.A." was originally composed in 1949 by Bess Lomax Hawes and Jacqueline Steiner as a campaign ditty for the Progressive Party's candidate for mayor of Boston, Walter O'Brien. (O'Brien lost to John Hynes.) In 2004, the MBTA introduced a new fare card, which they named "Charlie" in honor of the classic hometown anthem.

Turn right up Park Street, toward the State House.

In recent decades the building on the corner of Park and Beacon has housed various dining, café, retail, and media spaces. More than a century ago, however, the old **Amory-Ticknor House** was where author and educator **George Ticknor** (1791–1871) wrote his best-known work, *History of Spanish Literature*, over a period of two decades.

A cousin of William Ticknor's, of the Old Corner Bookstore, George began the first courses in Spanish and French literature and language at Harvard to supplement the traditional Greek and Latin. Among the best students in Ticknor's department were Henry David Thoreau, James Russell Lowell, John Lothrop Motley, Francis James Child, and Charles Eliot Norton. When Ticknor resigned from Harvard in 1835, his friend Henry Wadsworth Longfellow took his place.

Ticknor also helped found the Boston Public Library, donating his own extensive collection—some 18,000 volumes—to the fledgling institution. For fifteen months he traveled throughout Europe, at his own expense, purchasing books on behalf of the Boston Public Library. These travels not only helped inspire his students, but also enabled him to meet the great writers of the day, including Lord Byron and Madame de Staël.

If you're on foot, a brief side trip will prove worthwhile. As you face the gold dome of the State House, bear right onto Beacon to visit the **Boston Athenaeum**, discreetly set back at 10½. In 1851, with a collection of some 50,000 volumes, it was one of the five largest libraries in the nation. (Its main competitor was the Library of Congress.)

Incorporated in 1807 as a private reading room, library, and art museum, the Boston Athenaeum became a haven for artists, writers, and their well-bred Brahmin backers. One of the oldest cultural institutions and the largest membership library in North America, the

Athenaeum also helped establish Boston's Museum of Fine Arts in 1876, providing much of the museum's early artwork. The current building, designed by Edward Clarke Cabot, was opened in 1849.

One of the finest descriptions of the Athenaeum was written by the poet, essayist, and anthologist **David McCord** (1897–1997) in his gentle and witty book, *About Boston* (1948):

> *Number 10 ½ Beacon Street, overlooking The Granary Burying Ground—as every literate American knows—is the address of the Boston Athenaeum. Though not the oldest of stockholders' libraries in America, it is easily the most famous and prosperous of them all. . . . From 1822 to 1849 you would have found it down on Pearl Street. But it is in the present original and otherworldly building that the Athenaeum has grown in tradition and influence. No other Boston institution has anything like its unique, endearing, and enduring atmosphere. It combines the best elements of the Bodleian, Monticello, the frigate* Constitution, *a greenhouse, and an old New England sitting room. . . . The Athenaeum is a kind of Utopia for books: the high-ceilinged rooms, the little balconies, alcoves, nooks and angles all suggest sanctuary, escape, creature comfort. The reader, the scholar, the browser, the borrower is king.*

A repository for many important original works—from paintings and statuary to the book collections of George Washington and Henry Knox—the Boston Athenaeum has served prestigious scholars for almost two centuries. Typical among its nineteenth-century members was Ralph Waldo Emerson, who would take the train from his home in Concord, then visit the Old Corner Bookstore and the Athenaeum before dining at the Parker House. Less typical, perhaps, was **Nathaniel Hawthorne**, who communed with the polite ghost of one Reverend Thaddeus Mason Harris in the Pearl Street Athenaeum's reading room in 1842, while the specter was browsing over the *Boston Post*.

Harris was an industrious, wise, and withered man, whose lifetime had been spent ministering to his Unitarian flock in Dorchester, as well as joining the active ranks of groups like the Massachusetts Historical Society, the Humane Society, the Massachusetts Horticultural Society, and the Boston Athenaeum. On the day of Harris's death, however, Nathaniel Hawthorne began running into the late reverend's unsuspecting specter, couched in his customary chair near the fireplace in the Athenaeum's reading room. As he described it later, Hawthorne was baffled about what to do:

After a certain period—I really know not how long—I began to notice . . . a peculiar regard in the old gentleman's aspect towards myself. I sometimes found him gazing at me, and, unless I deceived myself, there was some sort of expectancy in his face.

. . . Being a ghost, and amenable to ghostly laws, it was natural that he was waiting to be spoken to before delivering whatever message he had to impart. . . . In the reading room of the Athenaeum conversation is strictly forbidden, and I could not have addressed the apparition without drawing the instant notice and indignant frowns of the slumberous old gentlemen around me. I myself, too, at that time, was as shy as any ghost, and followed the ghost's rule never to speak first.

Though long considered a bastion of conservatism, the Athenaeum has also been a gathering place for more than its share of nineteenth-century radicals and twentieth-century progressives.

In the 1820s, when women were often excluded from colleges and libraries, **Hannah Adams** (1755–1831), a distant relative of the statesman John Adams, was allowed to study here and was even granted full access by 1827. However, the woman heralded as America's first full-time professional female author was locked inside the library during lunch hours so she could pursue her studies "in modesty." Adams's popular works include *A Summary History of New England* (1799), *The Truth and Excellence of the Christian Religion Exhibited* (1804), and *The History of the Jews* (1812).

When **Lydia Maria Child** (1802–1880) wrote an immediatist anti-slavery tract, *An Appeal in Favor of That Class of Americans Called Africans* (1833), she found her Athenaeum privileges mysteriously revoked. And when that pamphlet was exhibited at Ticknor's Old Corner Bookstore, an irate crowd smashed the shop's windows. Boston society in the 1830s was not ready to embrace abolitionism—especially those who favored the *immediate* abolition of slavery—though its landscape would change dramatically in the next three decades.

Lydia Maria Child

Child was known by her contemporaries as a writer of abolitionist literature, romantic novels, household guides, and didactic fiction. Her best-selling romance novel, *Hobomok* (1824), for example, had an underlying theme of racial tolerance, while her popular book *The Frugal Housewife* (1829) guided married women to better household management.

Today Lydia Maria Child is remembered for less political work, notably her Thanksgiving verse from *Flowers for Children* (1844–1846):

Over the river and through the wood,
To grandfather's house we go;
The horse knows the way
To carry the sleigh
Through the white and drifted snow.

Another less than traditional early member was the cigar-smoking poet **Amy Lowell** (1874–1925)—who ordered 10,000 Manila cigars in 1915, anticipating a wartime shortage. Born in Brookline, Massachusetts, to the famed New England Lowells, Amy grew from an inveterate tomboy into a radical poet and popular celebrity. Given free rein of the Athenaeum from childhood, Lowell was in literary heaven. In 1912 and 1913, her discovery of the actress Ada Dwyer Russell, the revolutionary *Poetry* magazine, and a subsequent trip to Europe—where she encountered Ezra Pound and the new school of "imagist" poetry—solidified her commitment to verse. Over the next dozen years, she edited or wrote ten books of poetry as well as a biography of John Keats. Sought after as a speaker on both sides of the

Amy Lowell

Atlantic, Lowell was also the first woman appointed to a position of authority (the Board of Directors) at the Athenaeum. Her collection *What's O'Clock?* was awarded a Pulitzer Prize posthumously in 1926.

Writers and thinkers who currently frequent the Athenaeum range from established historians like David McCullough (*John Adams*) to popular novelists such as Stephen McCauley (*Man of the House*) and children's book authors Irene Smalls (*Don't Say Ain't*) and Tobin Anderson (*Feed*).

Historian **Walter Muir Whitehill** (1905–1978) was director and librarian of the Athenaeum from 1946 to 1973. A concerned citizen, Harvard-bred scholar, and chronicler of Hub history—who helped save the Old Corner Bookstore building from demolition in 1960—Whitehill wrote several accessible and well-researched books, including the centennial histories *The Boston Public Library* (1956) and *The Museum of Fine Arts* (1970). His 1959 study, *Boston: A Topographical History*, remains a classic of its genre.

Directly across from the Athenaeum, 21 Beacon is now a building of condominiums, with restaurants and convenience stores at street level. It was once the ornate and lovely **Bellevue Hotel**, where Louisa May Alcott periodically rented rooms over a sixteen-year period. A year after her blockbuster *Little Women* (1868) was published, Alcott stayed here while writing *Little Women, or Meg, Jo, Beth, and Amy*, *Part Second*. Sometimes she shared the Bellevue's "sky parlor" with other women reformers or let her younger sister May teach drawing in her apartments. The maternal grandparents of John F. Kennedy also rented an apartment suite here for a dozen years during the World War II era. Fifteen years before his election to the presidency, JFK occasionally stayed here when visiting family and running for Congress.

Kennedy's statue is a block away, in front of the State House.

Heart-leaves of lilac all over New England,
Roots of lilac under all the soil of New England,
Lilac in me because I am New England.

—AMY LOWELL, "LILACS," IN *WHAT'S O'CLOCK* (1925)

Continuing up Beacon Street toward the crest of old Beacon Hill, notice the large high-relief sculpture across from the State House. The **Robert Gould Shaw/54th Massachusetts Regiment Memorial** honors Colonel Shaw and his African American volunteer regiment, who lost their lives during the Civil War—a tale beautifully retold in the 1989 film *Glory*.

The 54th Massachusetts, the most famous black regiment of the Union Army, was formed shortly after President Lincoln issued the Emancipation Proclamation in January 1863. The unit's officers, initially all white men, were led by Colonel Robert Gould Shaw, a twenty-five-year-old Harvard dropout and the son of a prominent abolitionist family, who had already seen action at Antietam and Cedar Mountain.

Robert Gould Shaw/54th Massachusetts Regiment Memorial

John Greenleaf Whittier

Still, Shaw's African American soldiers—trained at Camp Meigs in Readville, near the modern neighborhood of Hyde Park—were, in the words of Governor John Andrew, "full of hope and glory." The 54th embodied the aspirations of northern blacks who sought to dispel racial stereotypes that black men could not be effective soldiers, and lay the foundation for their postwar claims of full citizenship. It was this regiment that would fight for pay equal to that of white troops and for the opportunity to rise within the ranks and become officers.

By the time Shaw and his finely tuned regiment of 1,000 marched through the streets of Boston on May 28, 1863, Shaw had already observed, "There is not the least doubt that we shall leave the State with as good a regiment as any that has marched." Throngs came out to cheer as the 54th filed past the State House, then marched down toward Battery Wharf, where the steamer *De Molay* waited to take them to battlefields in the South.

Many of New England's most progressive thinkers, writers, and abolitionists came together for this day of unity and community in Boston. Even the pacifist poet **John Greenleaf Whittier** attended, as he later wrote to Lydia Maria Child:

The only regiment I ever looked upon during the war was the 54th Massachusetts on its departure for the South. I can never forget the scene as Colonel Shaw rode at the head of his men. The very flower of grace and chivalry, he seemed to me beautiful and awful, as an angel of God come down to lead the host of freedom to victory.

Thirty-four years after the 54th's gallant rush on Fort Wagner, South Carolina—in which the colonel and many of his troops died—Boston paid tribute with this grand memorial. Among those who spoke at its

1897 dedication were Booker T. Washington, the founder and president of Tuskegee Institute in Alabama, and philosopher William James, whose brother Garth Wilkinson James had served as an officer under Shaw. (Another brother, Robertson James, served in the 55th Massachusetts, the second of the state's three black Civil War units.)

Sculpted by the eminent Augustus Saint-Gaudens, Boston's finest piece of public art (and the regiment itself) has inspired prose and poetry from the pens of James Russell Lowell, Ralph Waldo Emerson, Charles Ives, Luis Emilio, Lincoln Kirstein, Paul Laurence Dunbar, John Berryman, and many others. An excellent modern resource on both the regiment and the memorial, *Hope & Glory: Essays on the Legacy of the 54th Massachusetts Regiment* (2001), edited by historians Martin Blatt, Thomas Brown, and Donald Yacavone, was an outgrowth of the celebration of the memorial's centennial in 1997.

One of the most memorable and moving pieces about the memorial—from the tumultuous civil rights period of the 1960s—was Robert Lowell's "For the Union Dead" (1964):

> *Two months after marching through Boston,*
> *half the regiment was dead;*
> *at the dedication,*
> *William James could almost hear the bronze*
> *Negroes breathe.*
>
> *Their monument sticks like a fishbone*
> *in the city's throat.*
> *Its Colonel is as lean*
> *as a compass-needle.*
>
> *He has an angry wrenlike vigilance,*
> *a greyhound's gentle tautness;*
> *he seems to wince at pleasure,*
> *and suffocate for privacy.*

Though the **Massachusetts State House** is more closely associated with politics than pens, one particular event provoked an assemblage of literary greats on the steps below. The planned execution of the Italian immigrants Nicola Sacco and Bartolomeo Vanzetti in 1927

Boston Common and the
Massachusetts State House

aroused worldwide demonstrations of sympathy. Among those who adamantly protested the conduct of the trial and, ultimately, the electrocution were prominent writers Edna St. Vincent Millay, John Dos Passos, Dorothy Parker, and **Upton Sinclair** (1878–1968).

Sinclair's 1928 novel, entitled simply *Boston*, was based on the Sacco-Vanzetti trial—and banned in Boston by the ever-vigilant New England Watch and Ward Society. In intimate and intricate detail, Sinclair spun the tale of the two anarchists, whom he viewed as innocent victims of America's postwar xenophobia, the Red Scare of the 1920s, and a patently unfair legal process:

> *All day long the pickets would come, one batch after another, ten or twenty at a time, with their placards of polite protest, all bad words barred. They would walk their appointed number of paces, and then the police would close about them, and take them in tow, and march them . . . to the police-station. . . .*

> *There were well-known names among them. Edna St. Vincent Millay, from Rockland, Maine, home of her ancestors for many generations. Loveliest of woman poets, she would find this a devastating experience; life would not seem the same after a rendezvous with murder.*

Among the many public statues that grace the front of the State House are two free-thinking colonial women, Anne Hutchinson and Mary Dyer. Hutchinson was banished from Boston for her heretical views on religious freedom; Dyer, a practicing Quaker, was hanged by Boston Puritans for largely similar reasons.

For many years, the sculptures of Hutchinson and Dyer were the only two pieces of outdoor art in the city that depicted actual women (though idealized female forms representing Freedom, Faith, Knowledge, Art, Grief, and the like have long been favorite motifs).

Into the darkness they go, the wise and the lovely.
Crowned.
With lilies and with laurel they go; but I am not
resigned.

—EDNA ST. VINCENT MILLAY, "DIRGE WITHOUT MUSIC,"
IN *THE BUCK IN THE SNOW AND OTHER POEMS (1928)*

In the late 1990s, however, steps were taken to rectify this situation. In 1999, a dynamic bronze statue of Harriet Tubman—titled *Step on Board* and sculpted by Fern Cunningham—was installed in Harriet Tubman Park on Columbus Avenue. A new memorial representing three Boston women of letters—Phillis Wheatley, Abigail Adams, and Lucy Stone—and created by sculptor Meredith Bergmann, was dedicated on the Commonwealth Avenue Mall in October 2003, after more than ten years of preparation. Meanwhile, a project initiated by the Massachusetts legislature helped fund *Hear Us*, a public art installation by Sheila Levrant de Bretteville and Susan Sellers commemorating the contributions of women to public life and social justice in Massachusetts. A mixed-media portrait gallery featuring six women from Boston now lines the walls inside the left front entrance to the State House. Two of the women are known for their literary contributions, Lucy Stone and Josephine St. Pierre Ruffin.

An abolitionist, feminist, and popular orator, **Lucy Stone** (1818–1893) was one of the first women in Massachusetts to earn a college degree. When she married reformer Henry Brown Blackwell, she kept her maiden name. This radical act inspired other women to follow suit, earning them the nickname "Lucy Stoners." Stone cofounded and helped raise the funding for the *Boston Woman's Journal* in 1870, which became a weekly newspaper and major voice of the American Woman Suffrage Association.

Lucy Stone

Even in death, Stone was unusually modern for her time. She was cremated at the facility that is now part of Forest Hills Cemetery— one of New England's first cremations, performed in Boston's first, and only, crematory.

Josephine St. Pierre Ruffin (1842–1924), who lived on Charles Street, was the African-American publisher and editor of the *Woman's Era*, the first newspaper in America created by and for black women. A socially and politically active link between the city's wealthy white reformers and its African-American elite, Ruffin was a major player in the women's club movement and was associated with well-known reformers like Julia Ward Howe and Lucy Stone. A member of the New England Women's Press Association, Ruffin helped to establish the New Era Club for African-American Women and cofounded the National Federation of Afro-American Women, a precursor of the National Association of Colored Women.

Though today associated with landscaped paths, public monuments, ranger-led walks, concerts, festivals, ball games, street vendors, protests, a skating pond, an underground parking garage, and stops for subways and tourist trolleys, **Boston Common**—on the slopes below the State House—was once used for more unusual pastimes.

That forty-eight-acre stretch of common land, set aside by the town for shared use in 1634, was the first public green in America. It was thus a perfect site for Mary Dyer's hanging, which took place from the Great Elm that once stood here. The young Ralph Waldo Emerson was said to have grazed his mother's cows on the Common—a practice continued until 1830. Meanwhile, the relatively open Common served as a military training field, public burying ground, preacher's pulpit, scene of public punishment, deer park, and balloon launching pad, among other pursuits.

Poet David McCord summed up the Common's broad appeal in *About Boston* (1948):

> *Boston Common is an ancient battleground of ideas and beliefs and freedoms—unmarked by pyramids of cannon balls, unrelieved by crosses to the fallen, as void of redoubt as of the mischievous doubt in the worst ancestral skull. . . . The hanging of four Quakers simply for being Quakers is perhaps the darkest chapter. . . .*

It is impossible even to attempt a three-hundred-year summary of the uses to which the Common at large has been put. Emerson as a boy drove a cow to pasture there; and cows were not put on the Common black list until 1830. [Military drills], fireworks, kite flying, snipe shooting, carpet beating, Punch and Judy shows, telescopes, coasting, the long coast on what were called monster double rippers . . . Whig mass meetings, anti-slavery meetings, a railroad jubilee, promenade concerts, conventions, Indian dances, sermons, the secluded smokers' circle, three hundred spinsters spinning . . . the Common has seen, known, heard or been them all.

It's likely that every great literary figure who lived in or visited Boston once walked across the rolling acreage of the Common. The most famous pair to ramble here, however, may well have been **Walt Whitman** (1819–1892) and the adult Ralph Waldo Emerson.

Whitman espoused a literary eroticism—and, on occasion, homoeroticism—that gnawed at Victorian morals. Emerson invited Whitman on a lengthy walk across the Common in 1860 and tried to convince him to delete some of the racier passages from his 1855 opus, *Leaves of Grass*. Whitman did not waver, and the work was periodically banned throughout the country over the ensuing decades.

Walt Whitman

"Each point of Emerson's statement was unanswerable," observed Whitman, "no judge's charge ever more complete or convincing. I could never hear the point better put—and then I felt down in my soul the clear and unmistakable conviction to disobey all, and pursue my own way." Meanwhile, Emerson registered his esteemed colleague as a guest at the Boston Athenaeum.

Another nineteenth-century writer—the irrepressible **Oliver Wendell Holmes, Sr.** (1809–1894)—immortalized one particular walkway on the Common. The so-called Long Path runs from the

Oliver Wendell Holmes, Sr.

Guild Steps, where Joy Street meets Beacon, to the corner of Tremont and Boylston. Here, in his *Autocrat of the Breakfast Table* (1865), Holmes meandered with a certain schoolmistress:

At last I got out the question,—Will you take the long path with me?—Certainly,— said the schoolmistress,—with much pleasure.—Think,—I said,—before you answer: if you take the long path with me now, I shall interpret it that we are to part no more, and so it was.

Though educated in law and medicine—he was Harvard's first Parkman Professor of Anatomy and Physiology, dean of Harvard Medical School, and a founding member of the American Medical Association—Oliver Wendell Holmes was, quite literally, the man who made Boston "the Hub of the Solar System." He first used that phrase in his popular and amusing columns called "Autocrat of the Breakfast Table," most of which ran in the *Atlantic Monthly* and were later collected in book form. (His words were misquoted and remembered as "Hub of the Universe.")

Holmes's literary skills first came to light with his poem "Old Ironsides" (1830), which inspired Bostonians to save the historic USS *Constitution* from demolition. Though he published important medical works, it was his witty, urbane, poetic, and sometimes sentimental writing and public speaking that caught the public's attention. Holmes was not only a major contributor to the *Atlantic Monthly*, he was also the man who named it. When James Russell Lowell became the magazine's first editor in 1857, it was with the tacit understanding that Holmes would be a regular contributor.

In more recent years, Boston Common has been a pulpit for international personalities such as Pope John Paul II in 1979 and, nearly fifteen years earlier, the **Reverend Martin Luther King, Jr.** (1929–1968), who called for racial equality in a grand civil rights rally.

On April 23, 1965, some 50,000 people marched three miles, from Roxbury to the Common, to protest racial discrimination in the

*I have a dream that my four little children
will one day live in a nation where they will
not be judged by the color of their skin
but by the content of their character.
I have a dream today.*

—MARTIN LUTHER KING, JR., SPEECH GIVEN DURING
CIVIL RIGHTS MARCH ON WASHINGTON (1963)

northern as well as southern states. In his speech to this gathering, King declared:

I come not to condemn but to encourage. I would be dishonest to say Boston is Birmingham or that Massachusetts is a Mississippi. But it would be irresponsible for me to deny the crippling poverty and the injustices that exist in some sections of this community.

The grandson of a slave, King was a Baptist clergyman and leading civil rights activist committed to the style of nonviolent protest advocated by Mohandas ("Mahatma") Gandhi. His education included doctoral studies in systematic theology at Boston University between 1951 and 1955. In those years, King delivered sermons at a number of local churches, acquiring a reputation as a powerful and charismatic preacher. It was here that he gained inspiration and direction from the Reverend Howard Thurman—the first black chaplain at Boston University and the most influential black theologian of the twentieth century—and here where he began dating his future wife, Coretta Scott, a student at the New England Conservatory of Music.

Martin Luther King, Jr.

King's papers are among the treasures of Boston University's manuscript collections. His major books were collected sermons and essays, such as *Stride Toward Freedom* (1958), *Why We Can't Wait* (1964), and *Where Do We Go From Here?* (1967).

Directly across the Common, along Boylston Street, are two other notable sites. In a lodging house on the road once called Carver Street (now part of Charles Street South), **Edgar Allan Poe** was born in January 1809. Later that summer, Poe and his parents—both professional actors—moved to New York, though young Edgar returned to Boston in 1827 in search of literary fame.

One of Poe's eerie tales, "The Cask of Amontillado," had its origins in Boston. According to Edward Rowe Snow—known and loved for his storytelling histories of the Boston Harbor Islands—a sword duel took place on Castle Island, in South Boston, on Christmas Day 1817. In the brief encounter, a young Robert Massie was slain by the fort bully, Lieutenant Gustavus Drane ("Captain Green" in Snow's stories). Enraged by Massie's death, the other soldiers got Drane drunk, hauled him into the fort's dungeon, chained him down, and sealed up the vault. Soon after, a memorial was erected on the site for their slain friend, Massie. Ten years later, under the name Edwin A. Perry, Poe enlisted in the 1st Massachusetts Heavy Artillery at Castle Island. He saw the monument, heard the tale—apocryphal though it may have been—and the rest, as they say, is literary history.

In 1989 a plaque was put up at 176 Boylston Street commemorating Poe. Poe had a love-hate relationship with Boston and often referred to it as "Frogpondium," after the frog pond on the Common. A comment in his *Broadway Journal* typifies his ambivalent feelings about the Hub:

We like Boston. We were born there— and perhaps it is just as well not to mention that we are heartily ashamed of the fact. The Bostonians are very

Edgar Allan Poe

well in their way. Their hotels are bad. Their pumpkin pies are delicious. Their poetry is not so good. Their Common is not a common thing—and the duck pond might answer—if its answer could be heard for the frogs.

Several doors to the left of Poe's plaque is the gracious **Colonial Theater**, at 106 Boylston. This site was one home of the Boston Public Library before it moved to Back Bay in 1895. The blocks behind and next to the Colonial are considered Boston's Theater District. The most comprehensive history of playhouses, plays, playwriting, and actors in Boston is *Broadway Down East* (1978), a beautifully illustrated and highly readable tome by the acknowledged dean of Boston theater critics, **Elliot Norton**. (In 2003, the venerable Norton died at the age of 100, having written reviews of some 6,000 performances over a 48-year career.)

Continuing down Beacon Street, with the Common on your left, you are on the slope of Beacon Hill. The beautiful, exclusive homes on the beautiful, exclusive streets of Beacon Hill have long sheltered nationally known literati. Among the dozens of writers who have lived and worked here over the decades were Louisa May Alcott, Henry David Thoreau, and Sylvia Plath, as well as historians William Cooper Nell, Henry Adams, Francis Parkman, and William Hickling Prescott. It was on Charles Street, at the base of Beacon Hill, that Annie Fields and Sarah Orne Jewett held literary salons, and on Joy Street, on the north slope of the Hill, that the

Harriet Beecher Stowe, 1868

African Meeting House provided a platform for antislavery speeches, rallies, and writings. **Harriet Beecher Stowe** (*Uncle Tom's Cabin*, 1852) was a frequent guest at both places.

At this point, you can either follow the main route of the Literary Trail, down Beacon Street, or turn "Off the Beaten Path" for a walking tour of Beacon Hill.

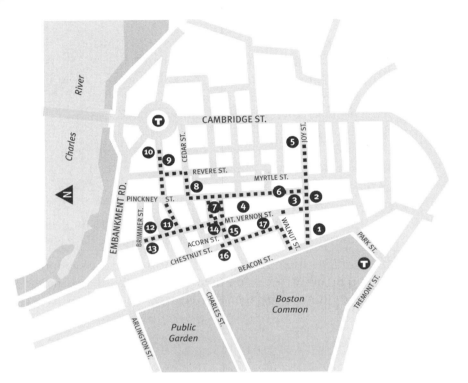

1. Former Little, Brown and Company headquarters
2. Beacon Press
3. Mount Vernon Street:
   Nichols House Museum (55)
   Henry Adams house (57)
   Thomas Bailey Aldrich house (59)
4. Club of Odd Volumes / Sarah Wyman Whitman House (77 Mount Vernon St.)
5. Joy Street/Smith Court:
   Abiel Smith School (46 Joy)
   William Cooper Nell house (3 Smith Court)
   African Meeting House (8 Smith Court)
6. Pinckney Street:
   Henry David Thoreau lodgings (4)
   Elizabeth Palmer Peabody kindergarten (15)
   Louise Imogen Guiney house (16)
   Alcott family lodgings (20)
   Louisa May Alcott lodgings (43 and 81)

   Old Phillips School (65 Anderson)
   Thomas Bailey Aldrich house (84)
   F. O. Matthiessen house (87)
7. Louisburg Square:
   John Gorham Palfrey house (5)
   William Dean Howells house (4 and 16)
   M. A. DeWolfe Howe house (16)
   Louisa May and Bronson Alcott house (10)
   Archibald MacLeish house
8. J. P. Marquand house
9. Lucretia Peabody Hale house
10. Site of James and Annie Fields house
11. Charles Street Meeting House
12. Henry (Sr.) and Alice James apartment
13. Samuel Eliot Morison house
14. Robert Frost house
15. Sylvia Plath apartment
16. Francis Parkman house
17. Julia Ward Howe house
    Radical Club

Beacon Hill: A Walking Tour
Approximate Time: 1 hour

Boston's first English settler was also the first colonist to inhabit the area now known as Beacon Hill. The **Reverend William Blackstone** (1595–1675), an Anglican expatriate from Robert Gorges's exploratory party of 1623, became a happy hermit here by 1625. The eccentric Blackstone contentedly rode about on his white bull and read from his collection of close to two hundred books—what might be called Boston's first library. Shortly after he invited John Winthrop's Massachusetts Bay Colony to share the Shawmut Peninsula, Blackstone left for less congested spaces.

The poet and novelist Conrad Aiken immortalized Blackstone in his 1947 poem, "The Kid":

Where now he roves, by wood or swamp whatever,
the always restless, always moving on,
his books burned, and his own book lost forever,
under the cold stars of New England, gone,

scholar who loved, and therefor left, the most,
secret and solitary, no Indian-giver,
who to his own cost played the generous host,
and asked adventurers across his river:

what would he make of us, if he could see,
after so many tides have ringed this coast,
what manner of men his children's children be,
to welcome home his still inquisitive ghost?

Meanwhile, Winthrop and his colonists renamed the peninsula Trimount, then Boston, and began creating systems to protect their young settlement from invasion. One such mechanism was a warning beacon set atop the peninsula's tallest hill. If intruders were spotted in the harbor, a bucket filled with tar was set aflame, and hiked to the top of a pole.

This area of Boston still bears names that reflect those days of early settlement. The hill, and later the street, were called Beacon. Trimount became Tremont. And one of the lesser of the three hills, Mount Vernon, was immortalized by a street name as well as by the Mount Vernon Proprietors, the group of five entrepreneurs who developed and built up this land at the end of the eighteenth century.

Begin your walking tour where Joy Street runs into Beacon, across from the Common. You'll note that the street first ascends the south slope, then descends the north slope of the Hill. The line between these slopes, not terribly apparent today, was significant for most of the nineteenth and early twentieth centuries.

While prosperous white families bought land and built elegant homes on the sunny southern slope overlooking Boston Common, their hired hands and unsightly outbuildings—servants, housemaids, stable boys, and stables—were often relegated to the congested, far less glorious back side of Beacon Hill. That north-south slope division also explains why so many persecuted and impoverished Eastern European Jewish immigrants and African Americans were able to live on Beacon Hill and in the adjacent West End throughout the nineteenth and into the early twentieth century.

In 1909, the house at 34 Beacon Street, at the corner of Joy Street, became the headquarters of **Little, Brown and Company**. Begun in 1837, when Charles C. Little and James Brown established Little & Brown, this publishing house was Houghton Mifflin Company's chief rival in Boston for several generations. Though it built a strong foundation with law books, Little & Brown won its first real literary acclaim with the nineteenth-century historic works of Francis Parkman.

Like Houghton Mifflin—whose offices were for many years at 4, then 2, Park Street—Little, Brown spent much of the twentieth century overlooking Boston Common. Although in different locations, both houses remain major international players to this day. Little, Brown is now part of the Time Warner conglomerate and has moved its editorial offices to New York.

As you walk up Joy to the corner of Mount Vernon Street, notice 41 Mount Vernon on the right. Once part of Little, Brown, it is currently the home of **Beacon Press**—though Beacon's official address is still 25 Beacon Street, at the Unitarian Universalist Association. Founded in 1854 (the name Beacon was not in general use until 1902), Beacon was considered a religious publishing house, owing to its connection with the Unitarian Church. Even in its first decades, however, Beacon began publishing works—eloquent writings on such topics as temperance, women's rights, abolitionism, and education of the working classes—that presaged the future direction of their publishing program. By the mid-twentieth century, Beacon had become synonymous with progressive social and political thought, and known for courageously printing important books and authors that other publishers were too timid to touch. It was at the forefront of those promoting black scholarship, world peace, education reform, the philosophies of the New Left, and feminist theology, and the first to publish books exposing the red-baiting Joe

McCarthy and the political clout of the Roman Catholic Church. Beacon authors also took aim at the war in Vietnam, making national headlines when they released the full text of *The Pentagon Papers* in 1971.

Take a short left onto Mount Vernon to view three impressive houses on the right.

At 55 Mount Vernon is the **Rose Standish Nichols House** and **Nichols House Museum**. A pacifist, pioneering garden designer, and international traveler, Rose Standish Nichols (1872–1960) left to posterity a beautiful home designed by Charles Bulfinch that offers a glimpse of the old Beacon Hill mansions. An originator of the Beacon Hill Reading Club and one of the founders of the Women's International League for Peace and Freedom, Nichols wrote three outstanding volumes about landscape architecture: *English Pleasure Gardens*, *Italian Pleasure Gardens*, and *Spanish and Portuguese Gardens*.

Next door, at 57 Mount Vernon, is the boyhood home of **Henry Adams** (1838–1918). A member of the Adams family of Massachusetts—which had already produced one framer of the Declaration of Independence, two U.S. presidents, and assorted congressmen, diplomats, and political crusaders—Adams was something of a lost soul. The work for which he is best known, *The Education of Henry Adams* (1907), explores his feelings of miseducation and his sense that he was snubbed by Boston society.

During the 1870s, Adams abandoned previous thoughts of a career in politics and became an assistant professor of medieval history at Harvard while editing the *North American Review*. Restless again, he moved to Washington, D.C., where he wrote the anonymous novel *Democracy* (1880), satirizing political corruption in the capital.

Though happily married to his beloved Marian Hooper in 1872, Adams fell into complete disarray following her suicide in 1885. Extended trips to the Far East, the South Pacific, and Europe allowed him to sidestep his sorrows periodically, and to devote himself to his nine-volume *History of the United States During the Administrations of Thomas Jefferson and James Madison* (1889–1891) and other scholarly works.

Henry Adams,
sketch by Samuel Lawrence

Despite much appreciation of his work, Adams's self-analysis was decidedly grim: "I want to look like an American Voltaire or Gibbon, but am slowly settling down to be a third-rate Boswell hunting for a Dr. Johnson."

Thomas Bailey Aldrich (1836–1907), editor of the *Atlantic Monthly* from 1881 to 1890, moved to the townhouse at 59 Mount Vernon in 1885 and remained here until his death. Though born in New Hampshire and raised in New Hampshire, New Orleans, and New York, Aldrich began his relationship with Boston when Ticknor & Fields published his book of poems *Blue and Gold* in 1865. An editing job at the illustrated journal *Every Saturday* brought him to the city that same year.

When not editing *Every Saturday* and the *Atlantic Monthly*, Aldrich was a journalist, poet, short story writer, and novelist. His best-known work was the semi-autobiographical *Story of a Bad Boy* (1873).

In *Memories of a Hostess*, Annie Fields recalled the curly-haired Aldrich as a bright, refreshing companion and curious fellow:

> He is a queer, witty creature. When the railroad dropped us at Green Lodge station . . . we found him sitting on a corner of the platform where he said he had been "listening to the bullfrog tune his violin. He had been twanging at one string a long time!" Aldrich was in an ecstasy of delight, and in truth it was a day to put the most untuned spirit into tune.

Farther down the street, at 77 Mount Vernon, is the mansion housing the **Club of Odd Volumes**, established in 1887 by a group of Boston men interested in promoting literary and artistic tastes, the exhibition of books, and social relations among its bibliophile members. Its Saturday lunches continue to this day for those interested in all facets of scholarship. A study of the group was done by Alexander Whiteside Williams in his *Social History of the Club of Odd Volumes* (1969).

The Club of Odd Volumes was originally lodged across the street, but moved into this townhouse in 1936. The home once belonged to artist **Sarah Wyman Whitman** (1842–1904), whose beautiful avant-garde book covers graced literary works by Thoreau, Hawthorne, Harriet Beecher Stowe, Celia Thaxter, and Whitman's close friend, Sarah Orne Jewett. Nationally known for her elegant simplicity of design, Whitman became the principal designer for Houghton Mifflin, creating some three hundred covers in all, and helping to define the art. Whitman was a multitalented artist, who also designed stained-glass windows for Trinity Church in Copley Square and Memorial Hall at Harvard.

Incidentally, 48 Mount Vernon was the address William Dean Howells chose for the fictional Coreys—the proper Bostonians who were duly shocked when poor Silas Lapham became inebriated at a dinner party in *The Rise of Silas Lapham* (1885).

Returning from Mount Vernon to Joy Street, begin your walk down Beacon Hill's north slope. On your left, 36A is a renovated carriage house and a well-maintained vestige of horse-and-carriage days. Turn left into Smith Court to see three important landmarks in Boston's black literary history.

At the corner, 46 Joy Street is the **Abiel Smith School**. Opened in 1835 as the first public school in Boston to educate African American children and the first building in the United States constructed for the sole purpose of housing a black public shool, the Abiel Smith became the battleground for the desegregation of Boston schools—a battle won, in theory at least, in 1855. Judge Lemuel Shaw presided over the original 1849 court case; he was the father-in-law of novelist Herman Melville. Thanks to federally funded renovations in the 1990s, the school opened as a museum space for the first time in Febrary 2000. It now houses the Museum of Afro American History's first permanent exhibitions and a museum store.

The double house at 3 Smith Court was once the home of **William Cooper Nell** (1816–1874), the black historian, writer, abolitionist, and leader in the school desegregation movement. The son of an early antislavery advocate and a close colleague of William Lloyd Garrison's, Nell worked his way up from errand boy to journalist and office manager at Garrison's abolitionist newspaper, *The Liberator*. Nell's most important book, *The Colored Patriots of the American Revolution* (1855), chronicled the accomplishments of African Americans that had not been previously documented. Its introduction was written by Harriet Beecher Stowe, the best-selling author of *Uncle Tom's Cabin* (1852).

The **African Meeting House**, at 8 Smith Court, is the oldest African American church built primarily by free black artisans still standing on its original site. Created as a place of worship, community center, and schoolroom for Beacon Hill's growing population of free blacks, the African Meeting House became both a symbol of hope and a landmark in black history. Together with the Smith Scool, it served as the nexus of the thriving free black community of nineteenth-century Boston. Most of the major abolitionist orators, activists, and writers spoke and rallied here in the decades before the Civil War. Prominent among the African American speakers were **Frederick Douglass** (ca. 1817–1895) and **Maria W. Stewart** (1803–1879).

Douglass was born Frederick Bailey, a Maryland slave, in 1817. When one of his early owners, Mrs. Hugh Auld, began teaching him to read, she

Frederick Douglass

was ordered by her husband to stop: "If [Frederick] learns to read," he warned, "it will forever unfit him to be a slave. He should know nothing but the will of his master, and learn to obey it." Auld did teach his slave to be a ship's caulker—a trade that came in handy when Frederick escaped from slavery and Baltimore in 1838, relocating to Massachusetts with his wife.

Shortly after his arrival, he changed his name to Douglass to make himself more difficult to trace. He also discovered *The Liberator*, William Lloyd Garrison's abolitionist newspaper. A powerful orator, Douglass spoke in pulpits ranging from the African Meeting House, Faneuil Hall, and Tremont Temple in Boston to halls throughout the British Isles. He published his own anti-slavery newspaper, *North Star*, and wrote three autobiographies, the best known of which is *Narrative of the Life of Frederick Douglass* (1845).

Douglass also worked at the African Meeting House to enlist soldiers for the 54th Massachusetts volunteers, who fought under Colonel Robert Gould Shaw. Two of Douglass's sons were among the 54th's first recruits.

In 1987, Boston writer and historian Marilyn Richardson recalled another significant voice associated with the African Meeting House in *Maria W. Stewart: America's First Black Woman Political Writer*. Stewart was an influential black activist, militant abolitionist, and defender of women's rights, now recognized as a significant forerunner of more familiar names like Frederick Douglass and Sojourner Truth.

The Liberator, masthead, 1859

Credited as the first American woman, black or white, to lecture publicly on political themes—and possibly the first black American to publicly espouse women's rights—Stewart's transcribed speeches became some of *The Liberator*'s earliest antislavery articles. Her religious meditations and lectures were compiled in pamphlets and volumes of collected works. Among her most compelling exhortations was a call for action to her black sisterhood, in the essay "Religion and the Pure Principles of Morality":

Ye daughters of Africa, awake! Awake! Arise! No longer sleep nor slumber, but distinguish yourselves. Show forth to the world that ye are endowed with noble and exalted faculties.

Walk back up Joy Street and turn right on Pinckney Street. On the left is 4 Pinckney, an apartment where **Henry David Thoreau** once lived.

A little farther on the right, 15 Pinckney is the site of one of several locations where **Elizabeth Palmer Peabody** held her kindergarten classes. Linked by family, friendship, and her own lifework to transcendentalism, major nineteenth-century authors, and innovative educators, Peabody combined her idealism with solid notions of educational reform in advocating a national system of kindergartens. Peabody, who also ran an influential foreign library and bookstore on West Street, is popularly known as the founder of the American kindergarten movement.

The Irish-American poet **Louise Imogen Guiney** (1861–1920) once lived at 16 Pinckney. A protégée and friend of Annie Fields and Sarah Orne Jewett, Guiney was the impoverished daughter of an Irish immigrant who grew into an established poet, essayist, and literary scholar, producing more than thirty books in her lifetime. Her most distinguished poetry and prose collections were *A Roadside Harp* (1893) and *Patrins* (1897). Heralded as "the Laureate of the Lost," Guiney was also committed to gaining recognition for obscure seventeenth-century Catholic English poets. Despite growing praise and admiration, her books sold poorly, forcing her to take a variety of jobs, including that of cataloger at the Boston Public Library. Her fans and friends came to include such contemporaries as Oliver Wendell Holmes, Jr., Thomas Bailey Aldrich, and Thomas Wentworth Higginson.

Though **Louisa May Alcott** usually had at least one home in Concord, she often maintained a pied-à-terre in Boston. A plaque on 20 Pinckney notes that Alcott was a little girl when her family rented this apartment; in actuality, she was twenty years of age. Alcott also rented rooms at 43 and 81 Pinckney—the latter overlooking Louisburg Square—and, at the end of her life, on Louisburg Square itself. Though Louisa had loved the town of Concord as a child, she felt far more at home in the city during her adult years.

At the corner of Pinckney and Anderson is 65 Anderson, with 1824 carved above its front door. Built as the **Phillips School**—one of Boston's finest centers for educating white children—it became one of the city's first integrated schools after the desegregation ruling of 1855.

Editor **Thomas Bailey Aldrich**, whom we met on Mount Vernon Street, made his first Boston home at 84 Pinckney.

Professor F. O. (Francis Otto) Matthiessen (1902–1950) lived at 87 Pinckney, also overlooking Louisburg Square. A Rhodes Scholar and graduate of Yale and Harvard, Matthiessen was a brilliant religious man and incisive literary critic. He was also an influential teacher at both his alma maters, and established the academic discipline now known as American Studies. Among his books are *Sarah Orne Jewett* (1929), *The Achievement of T. S. Eliot* (1935), *The James Family* (1947), and his pioneering study of nineteenth-century literature, *American Renaissance* (1941). Politically liberal and openly gay, Matthiessen was the longtime companion of painter Russell Cheney until the latter's death in 1945. At the dawn of the cold war and the McCarthy era, Matthiessen was persecuted for both his political opinions and his personal life. He committed suicide in 1950.

In her 1955 novel *Faithful Are the Wounds*, poet and novelist **May Sarton** (1912–1995) modeled her character Edward Cavan, a dedicated Harvard professor who committed suicide amid the McCarthy witch hunts, on F. O. Matthiessen. Though she was born in Belgium and died in her adopted home of York, Maine, Sarton spent much time in the area both living and working, giving her an insider's view of Harvard, Cambridge, and Boston.

The lovely private neighborhood lodged peacefully between Pinckney and Mount Vernon streets is **Louisburg** (pronounced *Lewisberg*) **Square**. Built between 1833 and 1847 as one of Boston's finest and most exclusive residential areas, it remains to this day an urban oasis, replete with a manicured park surrounded by an iron fence and handsome Greek Revival houses.

The strip of homes on the upper slope of the square has odd numbers. Unitarian clergyman **John Gorham Palfrey** (1796–1881), the author of numerous religious books, once lived at number 5. Palfrey is best remembered for editing the *North American Review,* a prestigious journal started in 1811 by the founders of the Boston Athenaeum. (The *Review,* as well as the *Atlantic Monthly,* were later purchased by James T. Fields of the Old Corner Bookstore.) Palfrey's five-volume *History of New England* (1858–1890) was a formidable work, well used and respected in his time.

Two of the even-numbered homes on the slope below the green—numbers 4 and 16—were rented by **William Dean Howells** (1837–1920), a novelist and editor of the *Atlantic Monthly,* between 1882 and 1884. Howells often discussed life and literature with colleague Henry James at number 16, and began writing his masterwork, *The Rise of Silas Lapham* (1885) there. We'll meet Howells again on the Literary Trail in Cambridge.

Number 16 was also the last home of editor, biographer, poet, and antiquarian **M. A. (Mark Antony) DeWolfe Howe** (1864–1960), who edited or authored an astonishing number of books on New England and Boston. Among his titles were *Boston Common: Scenes from Four Centuries* (1910), *Letters of Charles Eliot Norton* (1913), *The Atlantic Monthly and Its Makers* (1919), *Memories of a Hostess* (1922), and the Pulitzer Prize–winning *Barrett Wendell and His Letters* (1924). Though Howe was known for flattering and protecting his subjects—and, in his own daughter's words, was a "minor" writer—he created an irreplaceable mini-library of Boston history. He also edited the *Harvard Alumni Bulletin* and was affiliated in an official capacity with all the appropriate Brahmin institutions: Harvard College, the Boston Athenaeum, the Boston Symphony Orchestra, Trinity Church, the Tavern Club, and the Atlantic Monthly Corporation.

Louisburg Square

His daughter, novelist **Helen Howe** (1905–1975), chronicled Boston's nineteenth-century literary life in *The Gentle Americans* (1965).

The brightest literary lights on Louisburg Square were surely **Louisa May Alcott** (1832–1888) and her father, transcendentalist **A. Bronson Alcott** (1799–1888), who lived at 10 Louisburg Square from 1885 to 1888. Though long associated with Orchard House in Concord—where the family lived for almost two decades—the Alcotts were transient tenants at best, often forced to move when Bronson's progressive schools invariably failed. Especially after the success of *Little Women* (1868), Louisa proved a far better provider than her father.

As it turned out, Louisburg Square was the last home for both Louisa and Bronson. They both died in the spring of 1888, within two days of one another. Curiously, both father and daughter had been born on the same day—November 29—Bronson in 1799, and Louisa in 1832.

More contemporary authors who have lived on Louisburg Square include **Robin Cook** (b. 1940), the author of medical thrillers like *Coma, Brain*,

A poem should not mean
But be.

—ARCHIBALD MACLEISH, "ARS POETICA," IN *STREETS IN THE MOON* (1926)

Fever, and *Outbreak*, and Pulitzer Prize-winning poet and playwright **Archibald MacLeish** (1892–1982).

After serving in World War I and graduating from Harvard Law School (1919), MacLeish began to make his name in the world of letters. During the 1930s and 1940s he served in several government posts—Librarian of Congress and an assistant secretary of state under President Franklin D. Roosevelt—but literature was always his true calling. He was a prolific writer, trying his hand at experimental and socially progressive poetry, plays, prose, and verse drama. MacLeish was awarded Pulitzer Prizes in poetry for *Conquistador* (1932) and *Collected Poems, 1917–1952* (1952) and in drama for *J.B.* (1958), a modern retelling of the biblical trials of Job. In 1949 he became Boylston Professor of Rhetoric and Oratory at Harvard, a position he held until 1962.

Countless writers have immortalized Louisburg Square, including **Jean Stafford** (1915–1979), who captured its essence in her first novel, *Boston Adventure* (1944):

> *Her house was not far; its front windows faced Louisburg Square*
> *and here, as if it were an oasis chosen to delight the eyes of some*
> *favored heavenly power, the sun, hidden elsewhere by the city's*
> *smoke, shone brilliantly on white doorways and their brass trimmings.*

A novelist and short story writer, Stafford was born in California and raised in Colorado. *Boston Adventure* was the most popular of her novels, which included *The Catherine Wheel* (1952), *A Winter's Tale* (1954), and *Bad Characters* (1964). She also wrote a nonfiction account of the mother of Lee Harvey Oswald, *A Mother in History* (1966).

Stafford was the first (and the very unhappy) wife of Robert Lowell, who was raised at 91 Revere Street, just two blocks away. That address was immortalized in Lowell's satiric prose memoir of the same name in his confessional *Life Studies* (1959).

Return to Pinckney Street and follow it to West Cedar. Several doors down on the right is 43 West Cedar, where **J. P. (John Phillips) Marquand** (1893–1960) once lived. Marquand's first books were popular romances and detective stories; the Japanese detective Mr. Moto was one of his most

> *Marriage . . . is a damnably serious business,*
> *particularly around Boston.*
>
> —J. P. MARQUAND, *THE LATE GEORGE APLEY* (1937)

---

memorable characters. His greatest novel, however, was probably *The Late George Apley*, an insightful tale that gently satirized Boston's Brahmins and won the Pulitzer Prize in 1937.

It seems that Marquand was insecure when he first began writing *Apley*. After a friend in New York turned down the early manuscript, he asked Alfred McIntyre—another friend, and for years the head of Little, Brown—for a quick evaluation. "John, I think it is swell," McIntyre responded. "I can't tell you whether it will sell more than 2,000 copies—it may be too highly specialized. But by all means, go ahead with it!"

Turn left on Revere Street and go down to Charles Street, at the base of the Hill. The modern street numbers here differ from those of the nineteenth century. Keeping that in mind, walk along the right side of the street.

Lucretia Peabody Hale (1820–1900), a member of the illustrious Hale family—and the sister of Edward Everett Hale—lived at 127 Charles. A political progressive, Lucretia worked for women's rights and educational and social reform. Once a student in Elizabeth Peabody's school, she later helped start kindergartens and vacation schools while serving as one of the first women on the Boston School Committee. A contributor to the *Atlantic* from 1858, Hale is best known for her amusing books for children, especially *The Peterkin Papers* (1880), a collection of sketches about Bostonians' penchant for self-improvement.

Across the street, near the Charles Street Garage, stood that legendary gathering place of literary greats, 148 Charles Street. In *The American Scene* (1907), Henry James described "the waterside museum" of **James** and **Annie Fields** with appropriate awe:

> *Here, behind the effaced, anonymous door was the little ark of the modern deluge, here still the long drawing-room that looks over the water and towards the sunset, with a seat for every visiting shade, from far-away Thackeray down, and relics and tokens so thick on its walls as to make it positively, in all the town, the votive temple to memory.*

When James T. Fields of the Old Corner Bookstore moved here in 1856, the building was listed as 37 Charles Street; a decade later, it was renumbered 148. Regardless, its aura was absolutely stunning and the literary connections seemingly infinite. A typical encounter was remembered by Annie Fields in *Memories of a Hostess* (1922):

> *Dr. [Oliver Wendell] Holmes and his wife and Mr. [John Greenleaf] Whittier dined here. The talk was free, totally free from all feeling of constraint, as it could not have been had another person been present. Whittier says he is afraid of strangers, and Dr. Holmes is never more delightful than under just such auspices.*

Though James T. Fields died in 1881, the Charles Street salons did not die with him. Quite the contrary. Immediately after his death, a talented young writer from South Berwick, Maine, **Sarah Orne Jewett** (1849–1909), became Annie Fields's companion in a relationship that lasted the rest of their lives. Jewett's elegant and keenly observed stories of New England country life included *Deephaven* (1877), *Old Friends and New* (1879), *A Country Doctor* (1884), and her masterpiece, *The Country of the Pointed Firs* (1896).

As a young teenager in rural Maine, Jewett was inspired by Harriet Beecher Stowe's *Pearl of Orr's Island.* Convinced that sophisticated Bostonians vacationing in Maine did not appreciate the area's natural surroundings and simple, grand people, she determined to remedy that vision. At the age of nineteen, Jewett entered an illustrious literary circle when her first story was published in the *Atlantic Monthly,* thus beginning her lifelong association with the magazine and her vital connection to the Fields family. (In 1869, James T. Fields was still editor of the *Atlantic*.)

Committed in what was known as a "Boston marriage," Annie Adams

Sarah Orne Jewett

Fields and Sarah Orne Jewett were in the company of similar women of the late Victorian era. Alice James and Katharine Loring were life partners, as were sculptor Anne Whitney and Adeline Manning, poet Amy Lowell and Ada Dwyer Russell, and poet and educator Katherine Lee Bates (who wrote the lyrics to "America the Beautiful") and Katharine Coman. These liaisons—generally between wealthy professional women who could support themselves—were fairly well accepted by Boston society and treated socially as any other marriage. It's perhaps not surprising that the same region that condoned "Boston marriages" in the nineteenth century legally granted the right to same-sex marriage in the 21st century.

Perhaps because of their strong female bond, the Fields-Jewett salons were particular magnets for women writers and artists. Among those in attendance was the young **Willa Cather** (1873–1947), who observed and adored Fields and Jewett in her charming book *Not Under Forty* (1922):

> *Mrs. Fields wore the widow's lavender which she never abandoned except for black velvet, with a scarf of Venetian lace on her hair. She was very slight and fragile in figure, with a great play of animation in her face and a delicate flush of pink on her cheeks. Like her friend Mrs. John Gardner, she had a skin which defied age. As for Miss Jewett—she looked very like the youthful picture of herself in the game of "Authors" I had played as a child, except that she was fuller in figure and a little grey. I do not at all remember what we talked about. Mrs. Brandeis asked that I be shown some of the treasures of the house, but I had no eyes for the treasures, I was too intent upon the ladies.*

Turn around and head back toward the Common and the Public Garden. On the right, where Charles meets Mount Vernon, is 121 Mount Vernon.

Built in 1807 as a house of worship—a role it played for four consecutive congregations over 173 years—the **Charles Street Meeting House** was also a vibrant community center that witnessed meetings, educational forums, and spirited debates involving everyone from Sojourner Truth, Langston Hughes, Dr. Benjamin Spock, and leaders of the Beacon Hill Civic Association to members of feminist, gay, civil rights, arts, dance, and peace groups. The modest display that grew into the Museum of Afro American History began here, as did the groundbreaking *Gay Community News*, the nation's oldest gay newspaper (1973–1999).

Before man-made land separated the church from the river for several blocks, the Charles flowed up to the side of the brick meeting house, where River Street runs today. When nineteenth-century Baptists worshiped here, an underground opening on the river side apparently allowed baptism by immersion to take place inside the church without any fancy pumps or plumbing!

Continue walking down Mount Vernon. Number 131, on your right, was the home of **Henry James, Sr.**, and his daughter, **Alice,** for a brief period. **Henry, Jr.,** lived in some rooms at 102 Mount Vernon. The Jameses will reappear in the Cambridge segment of the Literary Trail.

Stop at the corner of Brimmer and Mount Vernon streets. The ivy-covered brick house on the left, 44 Brimmer, was the life-long home of **Samuel Eliot Morison** (1887–1976). Esteemed as a professor of American history at Harvard, an editor of the *New England Quarterly,* the official historian of the U.S. Navy during World War II, and a maritime historian par excellence, Morison's life here is best described in his brief yet eloquent memoir, *One Boy's Boston, 1887–1901* (1962).

At the turn of the last century, writes Morison, this area at the base of Beacon Hill was filled with sights, sounds, and smells quite different from those of today:

Almost the entire square between the backs of Beacon, River and Mt. Vernon Streets, and the river, was occupied by stables big and little— livery stables, which let out "sea-going" hacks and coupes; boarding and baiting stables, where gentlemen who drove in from the suburbs behind fast trotters left their rigs during the day; club stables where individuals could board one or two horses; dozens of private stables. Chestnut Street between Charles and the river was called "Horse-Chestnut Street" in derision. . . .

On Lime Street, there were at least two blacksmith shops, where the cheerful ringing of hammer on anvil could be heard from 7 A.M. to late afternoon. There was Chauncy Thomas's carriage factory on Lower Chestnut Street, where beautiful sleighs, victorias, broughams and other horse-drawn vehicles were built; Frederic J. Fisher, the famous body designer for automobiles, there had his training. . . .

My descendants will find it hard to believe that I once kept a horse at the Beacon Club Stable . . . and that even after becoming Professor Hart's assistant at Harvard I would combine business with pleasure by riding my grey gelding "Blanco" to Cambridge, tying him to a tree in the Yard, and loading the saddlebags with students' papers that had to be corrected.

Return to the corner of Charles Street and ascend Mount Vernon. As you turn right onto Willow Street, notice 88 Mount Vernon on the corner. **Robert Frost**—whom we'll encounter again in Cambridge—moved here in 1939.

Follow Willow Street to number 9, which faces the cobblestones of Acorn Street, perhaps the most photographed road in the city. Created as a back alley and filled with inexpensive rowhouses for servants and the less afflu-ent, Acorn Street is now a scenic delight. Tourists often aim their cameras up the street, apparently smitten with this tiny slice of old Boston.

In 1958, **Sylvia Plath** (1932–1963) moved to an apartment at 9 Willow while taking Robert Lowell's seminar at Boston University. Among her fellow students there were poets Anne Sexton and George Starbuck. Throughout her formal education—which included public schools in Winthrop and Wellesley, Massachusetts, followed by a scholarship at Smith College—Plath showed an aptitude for writing poetry and short stories. She also had a tendency toward anxiety, depression, paranoia, and suicide attempts, and she spent time as a patient at McLean Hospital, a psychiatric facility in Belmont, Massachusetts, after her junior year of college. Her stunning novel *The Bell Jar* (1963), first published under the pseudonym Victoria Lewis, described her junior-year suicide attempt.

Plath's depressed state had many sources, beginning with the death of her father when she was eight, and was apparently exacerbated by her troubled marriage to Ted Hughes, Britain's poet laureate. Her suicide in 1963, at the age of thirty, was prophetically alluded to in works like "Lady Lazarus" (1962):

Dying
Is an art, like everything else.
I do it exceptionally well.
I do it so it feels like hell.

Many of Plath's intensely personal poems, prose, and letters were published in posthumous collections, including *Ariel* (1966), *Crossing the Water* (1971), *Johnny Panic and the Bible of Dreams* (1977), and *Letters Home* (1975). Her *Collected Poems* (1981) was awarded a Pulitzer Prize.

Plath's classmate **Anne Sexton** (1928–1974) is generally considered her soulmate as well. Though Anne Harvey of Newton, Massachusetts, had written some poetry early in life, she wandered in other directions for several years—marrying Alfred M. Sexton II at nineteen, working as a fashion model and librarian, and raising two daughters. Discovering her talent for poetry became a personal salvation for Sexton, a way to ease her increasing anguish and perhaps ward off nervous breakdowns and suicide attempts. Beginning with her work in Robert Lowell's seminars, Sexton produced an impressive, self-exploratory body of work, including *To Bedlam and*

Anne Sexton

I would like a simple life
yet all night I am laying
poems away in a long box.

—ANNE SEXTON, "THE AMBITION BIRD" (1972)

Part Way Back (1960), *All My Pretty Ones* (1962), *The Death Notebooks* (1974), and the posthumously published *45 Mercy Street* (1976). Her accolades include a Pulitzer Prize, a National Book Award, and a Guggenheim Fellowship.

At forty-five, Sexton was found dead in an idling car in her Weston garage. Her fellow poet and friend Maxine Kumin, with whom Sexton wrote several children's books, explained to the press: "Life had a depressing effect on [Anne]. . . . Other times there were little notes or little warnings left about . . . but this time, no signs at all."

As Willow ends, take a right diagonal over to 50 Chestnut Street. As noted by its National Historic Landmark plaque, **Francis Parkman** (1823–1893) lived in this townhouse between 1865 and 1893. Born in Boston to a prominent family and educated at Boston Latin School, Harvard College, and Harvard Law School, Parkman was destined to become America's preeminent nineteenth-century historian. Despite chronic ill health—a nervous condition, severe vision impairment, and general exhaustion—he longed to write a "history of the American forest." Hence, at twenty-three, he and his first cousin Quincy Adams Shaw (who was himself the cousin of future Civil War colonel, Robert Gould Shaw) began an ambitious and rugged journey west from St. Louis, Missouri, to Wyoming. That trip, which included months spent with frontiersmen, pioneer settlers, and Native American tribes, culminated in Parkman's highly regarded opus, *The Oregon Trail* (1849).

Despite the popularity of his book, the year took its toll on the Parkman family. In the late fall of 1849, Francis's uncle George was murdered, dissected, and burned in a Harvard Medical School oven by John White Webster, a faculty member. The bizarre investigation and sensational trial that followed mortified the Parkman family and intrigued the world (including Charles Dickens, who requested a visit to the murder site on his subsequent American reading tour). Among those who testified at the trial was Dr. Oliver Wendell Holmes. The judge was Lemuel Shaw, the father-in-law of Herman Melville.

David McCullough on
Francis Parkman

I can never pass by Number 50 Chestnut Street on Beacon Hill, once the home of Francis Parkman, without an inner nod of gratitude. Few have written history with such sweep and flavor as did Parkman. In his hands, history became literature. And for someone raised in Pittsburgh, as I was, at the confluence of the Allegheny and Monongahela Rivers, where in the mid-eighteenth century the titanic French and Indian War began, there is little to equal the power of Parkman's *France and England in North America*, volume one of which, *Pioneers of France in the New World*, first appeared in 1865.

But what I am especially and everlastingly indebted to the great man for is a single paragraph in an introduction he wrote for a later edition of the book. To me it's gospel.

> *Faithfulness to the truth of history involves more than a research, however patient and scrupulous, into special facts. Such facts may be detailed with the most minute exactness, and yet the narrative, taken as a whole, may be unmeaning or untrue. The narrator must seek to imbue himself with the life and spirit of the time. He must study events in their bearings near and remote; in the character, habits, and manners of those who took part in them. He must be, as it were, a sharer or a spectator of the action he describes.*

Meanwhile, Francis Parkman's vision continued to deteriorate. With the assistance of readers and an instrument that helped him write with his eyes shut, Parkman—a consummate storyteller—created engaging narratives for the rest of his life. Among his major books are *History of the Conspiracy of Pontiac* (1851), the partly autobiographical *Vassall Morton* (1856), and the seven-volume *France and England in North America* (1865–1892).

Walk up Chestnut Street and cross over to numbers 13 to 15. These dwellings, designed by Charles Bulfinch, were built by Madame Hepzibah Swan, the only woman in the group of entrepreneurs that developed Beacon Hill. One of America's first art collectors, Swan gave these houses as wedding gifts for her three daughters.

The most illustrious resident at 13 Chestnut, however, was **Julia Ward Howe** (1819–1910), an abolitionist, poet, philanthropist, peace activist, feminist, social reformer, clubwoman, and mother of six. She also helped institute the original tribute to mothers in America, the very practical and political Mother's Day for Peace, begun in 1872. (Howe's concept of Mother's Day—as a pacifist plea for the world to stop killing their sons—failed to survive the century. The Mother's Day celebrated today, created by one Anna Jarvis, was first officially celebrated in 1914. Both Howe and Jarvis would surely be appalled by the overly sentimental and heavily commercialized version of modern times.)

Julia Ward Howe, 1868

Howe was well regarded as an editor of the abolitionist periodical *Commonwealth* and for her many contributions to the *Woman's Journal*. Her books included collected poems, travel sketches, an 1883 biography of Margaret Fuller, and her own *Reminiscences* (1899). Her undying fame, however, is a result of her impassioned text to "The Battle Hymn of the Republic."

The tune behind Howe's lyrics began as a vintage camp song, "Say, Brothers, Will You Meet Us," which was copied by members of the 12th Massachusetts Infantry for their new marching song, "John Brown's Body." Visiting Washington, D.C., during the early years of the Civil War, Howe heard the Bay State regiments singing "John Brown's Body" as they filed down the avenues. Smitten by the catchy music, she had her carriage chase after the soldiers. After borrowing the tune, the chorus, and an image or two, Howe's anthem was born—and published in the *Atlantic Monthly* in February 1862:

> *Mine eyes have seen the glory of the coming of the Lord;*
> *He is trampling out the vintage where the grapes of*
>   *wrath are stored;*
> *He hath loosed the fateful lightning of His terrible, swift sword;*
> *His truth is marching on.*

Abraham Lincoln reportedly wept when he first heard the hymn. Mrs. Howe was paid five dollars by the *Atlantic*.

The Swan houses continued to harbor innovative thought when Mrs. John T. Sargent moved in. From 1867 to 1880, 13 Chestnut served as a meeting place for the **Radical Club,** a group of daringly modern women and men that Sargent helped found. The liberal Unitarians who gathered here for discussion and debate included the home's former resident Julia Ward Howe as well as John Greenleaf Whittier, Ralph Waldo Emerson, Lydia Maria Child, Elizabeth Palmer Peabody, Thomas Wentworth Higginson, William Lloyd Garrison, and even Louisa May Alcott, when she was residing on Beacon Hill.

Continue up Mount Vernon and turn right onto Walnut. The main auto route of the Literary Trail resumes at the corner of Walnut and Beacon streets.

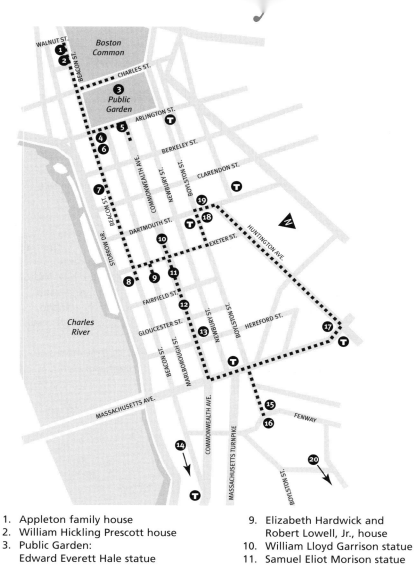

1. Appleton family house
2. William Hickling Prescott house
3. Public Garden:
   Edward Everett Hale statue
   Make Way for Ducklings sculpture
4. Former headquarters of the *Atlantic Monthly*
5. Boston Center for Adult Education
6. Gibson House Museum
7. Isabella Stewart Gardner's first house
8. Oliver Wendell Holmes house (296)
   William Dean Howells house / George Santayana house (302)

9. Elizabeth Hardwick and Robert Lowell, Jr., house
10. William Lloyd Garrison statue
11. Samuel Eliot Morison statue
12. Boston Women's Memorial
13. Fannie Farmer apartment
14. Eugene O'Neill apartment
15. Massachusetts Historical Society
16. John Boyle O'Reilly bust
17. Mary Baker Eddy Research Library
18. Boston Public Library
19. Kahlil Gibran monument
20. Forest Hills Cemetery

Return to the main route of the literary trail.

Immediately on your right is 39 Beacon Street, the **Appleton** family home, where daughter Fanny married Henry Wadsworth Longfellow in 1843. They will be visited again on Brattle Street in Cambridge.

The museum at 55 Beacon, marked by a commemorative plaque, is the former home of historian **William Hickling Prescott** (1796–1859). Like fellow historian and neighbor Francis Parkman, Prescott was plagued by damaged eyesight. While studying at Harvard, he had been hit in the eye with a crust of bread. Despite one blind eye and a second one weakened by iritis (arthritis of the eye), Prescott was determined to pursue a literary career. By 1826, however, he had shifted his sights from literary criticism to history.

For ten years, Prescott committed all his faculties to writing a three-volume history of the reign of Ferdinand and Isabella of Spain. Buoyed by its success, he went on to write *History of the Conquest of Mexico* (1843) and *History of the Conquest of Peru* (1847).

Among his international coterie of fans was Charles Dickens, whose letter to one Professor Felton was reprinted in James T. Fields's *Yesterdays with Authors* (1871):

I wrote to Prescott about his book, with which I was perfectly charmed. I think his description masterly, his style brilliant, his purpose manly and gallant always. The introductory account of Aztec civilization impressed me exactly as it impressed you. From beginning to end, the whole history is enchanting and full of genius.

At the base of the hill is Charles Street. Near the Charles Street gate to Boston's beautiful 24-acre **Public Garden** is a statue of writer, Unitarian minister, and reformer **Edward Everett Hale** (1822–1909), created by Bela Pratt and erected in 1913. Hale is best remembered for his classic patriotic tale *The Man Without a Country* (1863). Contemporaries, however, knew him also for his role at the turn of the twentieth century. On December 31, 1900, the seventy-eight-year-old Grand Old Man of Boston stood on the steps of the State House, faced a reverent and quiet crowd, and welcomed in the New Year— and new century—with a reading of Psalm 90.

A grandnephew of Revolutionary War patriot Nathan Hale, Edward entered Harvard College at age thirteen and graduated four years later as class poet and a member of Phi Beta Kappa. His wife, Emily Baldwin Perkins, was a niece of Harriet Beecher Stowe's. When not writing, lecturing, and pursuing political causes—including world peace and abolition—Hale led Boston's South Congregational Church, where he preached for forty-three years.

Not far from the statue is one of the most popular pieces of outdoor sculpture in the city. *Make Way for Ducklings*, a depiction of Mrs. Mallard and her eight ducklings by Newton artist Nancy Schön, was installed in 1987 to mark the 150th anniversary of the Public Garden. The shine on the bronze quackers' backs is from the countless children who lovingly play on them daily. The inspiration for this sculpture—*Make Way for Ducklings* by **Robert McCloskey** (1914–2003)—has been a children's classic since it was first published in 1941. (By the way, the original Quack, which was stolen and then recovered, resides in the Rey Children's Room of the Boston Public Library).

McCloskey's simple, timeless story, set in Boston, chronicles the trials of Mr. and Mrs. Mallard as they search for a nice place to live with their ducklings. The author and illustrator studied mallard ducks in museums and libraries before creating his drawings. To perfect his understanding of their habits and movement, McCloskey bought four live ducks from a poultry dealer, took them to his apartment, and followed them about for weeks with tissues and sketchbook in hand.

Stories and verse for children and young teens have always been part of Boston's literary picture. The subject of children's literature is a book in itself, but it's easy to get a glimpse of the role Boston and Bostonians played in this genre.

In the eighteenth century, **Thomas Fleet** (who may or may not have published Mother Goose's *Melodies*) did print the 1737 edition of *The New England Primer*. It was the first volume in which the children's prayer "Now I lay me down to sleep" was reproduced.

During the nineteenth century, Boston-bred **Horatio Alger, Jr.** (1832–1899), made his rags-to-riches tales a part of American culture, with dozens of redundant boys' books about Ragged Dick, Tattered Tom, and kindred spirits. Meanwhile, one of America's most popular series of "juveniles" (magazines oriented to young people), the *Peter Parley* books, were prepared with the aid of **Epes Sargent** (1813–1880), the editor of the *Boston Transcript*, who also compiled school readers.

Louisa May Alcott's *Little Women*, of course, has been the classic for girls since its publication in 1868. Alcott, like many of her contemporaries, also contributed stories to nineteenth-century "juveniles." The woman who helped save Alcott's Orchard House and The Wayside—Harriett Mulford Stone Lothrop (1844–1924), using the pseudonym **Margaret Sidney**—created her own children's favorites, the *Five Little Peppers* series. (The Alcotts and Sidney will be visited in greater detail in the Concord segment of the Literary Trail.)

Though **Nathaniel Hawthorne** (1804–1864) and **Henry Wadsworth Longfellow** (1807–1882) are not known primarily as children's authors, many of their works were committed to memory by generations of American youth. Longfellow's poems are also credited with generating a pantheon of heroes—from Paul Revere and Hiawatha to Miles Standish and the Village Blacksmith—that had been lacking in American culture. At the end of the century, **W. Gilbert Patten** (1866–1945), under the name Burt L. Standish, turned out a series of books about Frank Merriwell, everyone's favorite star athlete, gentleman, and All-American boy.

By the twentieth century, children's books were well on their way to becoming big business. Many of these books were written in the Greater Boston area by authors who found the city a good setting. Among them are **Kathryn Lasky** (*I Have an Aunt on Marlborough Street* and *She's Wearing a Dead Bird on Her Head!*), **Esther Forbes** (*Johnny Tremain*), **Margret** and **H. A. Rey** (the *Curious George* books), **E. B. White** (*The Trumpet of the Swan*), **Maxine Kumin** (*When Grandmother Was Young*), **Norma Farber** (*As I Was Crossing Boston Common*), **Lois Lowry** (*Taking Care of Terrific*), **Blair Lent** (*Molasses Flood*), **Jan Marino** (*The Mona Lisa of Salem Street*), **Ann Rinaldi** (*The Fifth of March*), **Shirley Graham Du Bois** (*The Story of Phillis Wheatley*), **Michael Emberley** (*Ruby*), and **Stephen Krensky** (*A Ghostly Business*).

Boston's **Public Garden** has been a source of joy for children for well over a century. The Swan Boats in particular—started by Robert Paget in 1877 and still run by his descendants—have been the stuff of memory. **Elizabeth Bishop**, for example, was so impressed by her Swan Boat ride here in 1914, at the tender age of three, that she vividly recalled it for the rest of her life.

Born in Worcester, Massachusetts, Bishop (1911–1979) was orphaned early in life and raised by a grandmother. Though she lived

Robert Pinsky on Elizabeth Bishop

Boston's waterfront was only beginning its great rebirth when Elizabeth Bishop moved to her apartment on Lewis Wharf, in a splendidly restored former warehouse building of gray stone. The architect had left elegant reaches of exposed, ancient beams visible in the corridor, recalling the ships and shipping of the building's history, and in Elizabeth's apartment, among works of art and memorabilia from her long residence in Brazil, a carved figurehead maiden spread her wings. The building, reaching its massive, flinty rectangle out to Boston Harbor, seemed right for her restless, traveller's spirit. Her childhood was spent in Worcester and in Nova Scotia: the North End with its hermetic, winding streets opening suddenly to water views seemed to distill that ocean-saturated Canadian landscape and the domestic streets.

Before I knew her, before the Lewis Wharf days, Elizabeth Bishop lived for a time virtually in Harvard Square, in an apartment on Brattle Street. The building was marked by a small neon sign, cursive letters identifying it as the "Brattle Arms." The silly, old-fashioned name, a kind of vulnerable glamour or sophistication in the script, evoke for me another side of Bishop, her urban poems like "The Man-Moth" and "Varick Street." This side of her, utterly non-academic, urbane and unpedantic, seemed to belong in the North End, but when she was in Cambridge she made it that much less a mere college town, that much more part of the great world of sights, tastes, sounds, smells and textures—the world well represented by the coziness and adventure of a harborside.

in this area for many years—first as a child, then later when hired to teach at Harvard and MIT—she also made her home in Nova Scotia, Greenwich Village, Key West, San Francisco, and Brazil. During her last year of study at Vassar College, Bishop met Marianne Moore, who became a significant mentor and friend, as did Robert Lowell more than a decade later.

First published in 1925 in an anthology introduced by Moore, Bishop was chosen Poet Laureate (then called Poetry Consultant at the Library of Congress) in 1949. By 1956 she had won the Pulitzer Prize for her book *Poems—North & South*, and by 1961 she was traveling down the Amazon River with Aldous Huxley. While her own true loves were women—most notably a Vassar classmate and a Brazilian aristocrat—Bishop was adored by Robert Lowell. In "For Elizabeth Bishop 4," Lowell mused on the extraordinary length of time it took his friend to perfect her poems:

Do
you still hang your words in air, ten years imperfect;
joke-letters glued to your cardboard posters, with gaps
and empties for the unimaginable phrase —
unerring muse who scorns a less casual friendship?

You are now on the corner of Beacon and Arlington streets. The latter is the first of the alphabet streets—Arlington, Berkeley, Clarendon, Dartmouth, Exeter, Fairfield, Gloucester, and Hereford—which cross this beautiful old neighborhood of lengthy avenues, known as the **Back Bay.** From colonial times through the early nineteenth century, it was indeed an estuary (not really a "bay," though the name persists), flooded by the Charles River during high tide, then reduced to odiferous mudflats when the tide ebbed. The space from the base of Boston Common through today's Public Garden was a beach, where residents swam, fished, and went boating, then clammed (or complained) when the tide was low.

The young Ben Franklin was among the many anglers here in the early eighteenth century. The British regulars who later camped out on the Common had yet another "angle": on the night of April 18, 1775, they boarded their boats for Cambridge, then marched on to Lexington and Concord while two lights flashed in the steeple of the Old North

Church, warning patriots of their approach. Longfellow took poetic license in describing this episode in "Paul Revere's Ride" (1863):

One if by land, and two if by sea;
And I on the opposite shore will be,
Ready to ride and spread the alarm
Through every Middlesex village and farm.

The "sea," of course, was the Charles River. And since there were no bridges, the Redcoats' only other route would have been the long stretch down today's Washington Street and through Roxbury.

Between 1857 and 1890, a major land-making project eliminated the old tidal flats. Though Bostonians originally called this reclaimed area "the New Land," the name Back Bay was in popular use by the 1870s. Meanwhile, a real estate boom replaced that former murk with fine homes and a variety of cultural institutions. One was the seminal *Atlantic Monthly*, which made its headquarters at 8 Arlington Street, on the corner of Arlington and Marlborough streets. Conceived at a Parker House gathering of the Saturday Club—a group that included Emerson, Longfellow, James Russell Lowell, and Holmes—the *Atlantic* began as a progressive Brahmin literary showcase, a self-proclaimed "journal of literature, politics, science, and the arts." Its first editors included **James Russell Lowell** (1857–1861), **James T. Fields** (1861–1871), and **William Dean Howells** (1871–1881).

Ellis Grey Loring, "Beacon Street"

When it made its debut in 1857, the *Atlantic* was boldly attempting to define and mold a distinctive American voice. From that time through the present it has been, among other things, a showcase for authors of note. Nathaniel Hawthorne sent in articles from the Civil War battlefront, and Julia Ward Howe offered her "Battle Hymn of the Republic." Felix Frankfurter made a plea on behalf of Sacco and Vanzetti, and Martin Luther King, Jr., presented a handwritten draft of his "Letter from Birmingham Jail." Many writers saw

*The continuity of glass constituted a kind of exposure,
within and without, and gave [Beacon] street an appearance
of an enormous corridor, in which the public and the private
were familiar and intermingled. But it was all very cheerful
and commodious, and seemed to speak of diffused wealth,
of intimate family life, of comfort constantly renewed.*

—HENRY JAMES, *A NEW ENGLAND WINTER* (1884)

their first printed stories on the pages of the *Atlantic,* including Henry James, Mark Twain, Louise Erdrich, Sue Miller, and Bobbie Ann Mason. In 1989, the *Atlantic* moved to Boylston Street, then to its current home, 77 North Washington.

Just around the corner from the old *Atlantic*, at 5 Commonwealth Avenue, is the house built in 1912 for Walter C. Baylies, a textile manufacturer. Now the **Boston Center for Adult Education**, it sponsors a broad spectrum of courses, including writing classes, seminars, and lectures by noted authors, poets, and journalists. In the 1950s, for example, poet **John Holmes** (1904–1962) taught a writing class here to a group that included Anne Sexton.

Beacon Street itself was called "the sunny street that holds the sifted few" by one resident, Dr. Oliver Wendell Holmes. Few private owners can afford these grand mansions today, though many of them have been bought by educational institutions. On this stretch of Beacon, you'll find many doors marked **Fisher College** and **Emerson College**.

Still, the well-preserved **Gibson House**, a National Historic Landmark at 137 Beacon, is a museum that gives visitors a glimpse of opulent Victorian Boston at its finest. The first row house built on the south side of Beacon between Arlington and Berkeley streets, the Gibson House is a fine example of the Back Bay during Boston's literary Golden Age. While the facade of the house features beautiful work by Edward Clarke Cabot—the same architect who designed the Boston Athenaeum—the interior offers nineteenth-century furnishings, books, and technological innovations, paintings, and photographs.

Constructed in 1859 and occupied by three generations, the house opened as a museum in 1957, following the death of **Charles Hammond Gibson, Jr.** (1874–1954). Gibson was a poet, author, horticulturist, and wonderfully curious character who carefully preserved his manuscripts in the hopes that scholars might later study them. He wrote many poems honoring British royalty, as well as lighter odes, such as those to a toad ("Hop, hop, sagacious toad!"), a worm, and a turkey. Several of his poems are framed and hang on the Gibson House walls; the expansive book collection includes multiple copies of his books of poetry and travel. Since 1974, the house has also served as headquarters for the New England Chapter of the Victorian Society in America.

Most people associate the legendary art collector and patron **Isabella Stewart Gardner** (1840–1924) with her palatial home in the Fens, but a plaque near 150 Beacon Street, on the right side of the street, marks the site of her first home in Boston. Years before she built Fenway Court—now the Gardner Museum—the charming and controversial "Mrs. Jack" lived at 152 Beacon, between Berkeley and Clarendon streets. After the deaths of her only son, her husband, and a variety of relatives, Gardner was left with a lot of sorrow—and a lot of money.

She also had a great deal of good sense and surrounded herself with Boston's cultural elite as well as some of its most celebrated Bohemians. When not mixing with the likes of Henry James, Henry Adams, James McNeill Whistler, John Singer Sargent, and Charles Eliot Norton, Gardner was busy sending a young Harvard student (Class of 1887) on art-buying expeditions throughout Europe. This protégé was **Bernard Berenson** (1865–1959), who became an internationally known art historian and critic and *the* connoisseur of Renaissance art. His many books and monographs on Renaissance art and art appreciation were penned with consummate grace, knowledge, and style.

One of the scandalous aspects of Mrs. Jack's life was her wealth of male admirers, who buzzed about when her husband was alive. Though most scholars doubt that these liaisons were ever consummated, her relationship with popular author **F. Marion Crawford** (1854–1909) may well have involved an affair. The son of sculptor Thomas Crawford and nephew of Julia Ward Howe, he published some four dozen romance novels, known for little more than their international settings and entertainment value.

Notice that the street numbers here skip from 150 to 154. That gap was created at the pleasure of Mrs. Gardner, who mandated that "her" number 152 never be used on Beacon Street once she had moved.

Continue on Beacon to Exeter Street. Before turning left onto Exeter, look halfway down the right-hand side of the Exeter-Fairfield block. Here, at 296 Beacon, **Oliver Wendell Holmes, Sr.**, spent the last twenty-three years of his life. Though born in Cambridge near Harvard Square and a resident of Charles Street for many years, he moved to Beacon Street in 1871, where he entertained both people of medicine and people of letters.

Three doors down is 302 Beacon, yet another residence of *Atlantic Monthly* editor **William Dean Howells**—a gentleman we've met in Louisburg Square and will meet again at the house he built in Cambridge. Howells moved here in 1885, the year his novel *The Rise of Silas Lapham* was published.

From 1872 to 1881, 302 Beacon was also home to a Spanish American youth named **George Santayana** (1863–1952). Santayana studied at Boston Latin School and Harvard College—where he was a student of William James—and eventually gained renown as a Harvard instructor (1889–1912), philosopher, poet, literary critic, humanist, and author of *The Sense of Beauty* (1896), *The Life of Reason* (1905–6), and other works. Feeling the perennial outsider in Boston and Cambridge society, he moved to Europe in 1912. It was there that Santayana wrote his only novel, the best-selling *The Last Puritan* (1935), a biting satire of late nineteenth-century Boston that drew on his own experiences with—and disappointments in—Proper Bostonians and their culture.

Turning up Exeter, you'll come to Marlborough Street. About halfway down the street on your right is 239 Marlborough, where Robert Lowell moved with his second wife, critic and novelist Elizabeth Hardwick, in 1955. **Robert Lowell, Jr**. (1917–1977), found life in the twentieth century—and life as a member of the venerable Lowell clan—an uncomfortable fit. A rebel by nature, he transferred from Harvard to Kenyon College, converted to

Robert Lowell

Catholicism, and became a conscientious objector during World War II. After spending several months in jail as a result, he published his first collection of poems, *Land of Unlikeness,* which won the Pulitzer Prize when it was expanded into *Lord Weary's Castle* (1945).

In the early and mid-1950s Lowell foundered, regaining his vision and direction partly with the help of contemporaries like Allen Ginsberg and William Carlos Williams, and partly through psychiatric care at McLean Hospital in Belmont, Massachusetts. By the end of the decade, he was teaching at Boston University—where his students included Sylvia Plath and Anne Sexton—and publishing his master-work, *Life Studies* (1959). Both it and his powerful "For the Union Dead" (1964) placed Lowell at the head of the new breed of confessional poets in America.

Between 1949 and 1972, Lowell was married to **Elizabeth Hardwick** (b. 1916), the second of his three wives. Born in Kentucky, Hardwick, like her husband, was disenchanted with Boston in the 1950s. In her essay "Boston: The Lost Ideal" (1959), she mused on her theory that the city's period of intellectual superiority was long gone:

Boston—wrinkled, spindly-legged, depleted of nearly all her spiritual and cutaneous oils, provincial, self-esteeming—has gone on spending her inflated bills of pure reputation decade after decade. Now, one supposes, it is over at last.

Hardwick and Lowell subsequently transplanted to New York City. In her essay "The Genius of Margaret Fuller" (1986), Hardwick saw this escape route—savoring what little Boston had to offer, then moving on to Manhattan—similar to that of the brilliant Fuller more than a century before:

[Margaret Fuller] was born in the wrong place, the place thought to be the only right one for an American intellectual in the nineteenth century. That is, she was born in Cambridgeport, Massachusetts, around Harvard, Boston, Concord, and all the rest. She sprang out of the head of all the Zeuses about: her father Timothy Fuller, Emerson, Goethe. . . . [W]hat the whole span of her life shows is that she got all from being around Boston at the transfiguring moment, and would have lost all had she not escaped.

*I am in earnest—I will not equivocate—
I will not excuse—
I will not retreat a single inch;
and I will be heard!*

—WILLIAM LLOYD GARRISON, *THE LIBERATOR* (1831)

Where Exeter crosses Commonwealth Avenue, you will find two significant men of action and letters seated on the left and the right of the Mall.

On the left you see the back of the abolitionist **William Lloyd Garrison** (1805–1879). Dedicated in 1886, this bronze statue by Olin Levi Warner was the first seated memorial on the Mall. Abandoned by a seafaring father, then raised by a poor deacon in Newburyport, Massachusetts, Garrison learned the newspaper trade as a youth. As editor of the *Free Press,* he was the first to publish the poems of John Greenleaf Whittier. Once committed to abolitionism, Garrison risked his life and livelihood by founding the New England Anti-Slavery Society and the American Anti-Slavery Society, and publishing his unapologetic and outspoken newspaper, *The Liberator.*

Though many of his peers preferred to fight slavery with an entourage of white males, Garrison believed that women and African Americans were as important to the cause—and to his newspaper—as any privileged Brahmin. Garrison's wise face looks worn in Warner's bronze, but his hand grasps a bundle of papers with strength and conviction. It's a tribute to his progressive thinking that a man who was chased by a lynch mob through the streets of Boston in 1835 would be memorialized there only half a century later.

William Lloyd Garrison,
Commonwealth Avenue Mall

The seated sculpture facing you from the Exeter-Fairfield block is maritime historian **Samuel Eliot Morison** (1887–1976), whom we met at his home near Charles Street. The piece, created by Penelope Jencks, was added to the Mall in 1982. Perched on a twenty-ton granite boulder, the native Bostonian and U.S. Navy admiral was a sailor, Harvard professor, prolific author, and Pulitzer Prize winner. Among his best-known books are *Builders of the Bay Colony* (1930), *The Founding of Harvard College* (1935), *The Growth of the American Republic* (1930, with Henry Steele Commager), and *The Oxford History of the American People* (1965). His Pulitzer Prizes were awarded for biographies: *Christopher Columbus, Admiral of the Ocean Sea* (1942) and *John Paul Jones* (1959).

One block farther, on the Fairfield-Gloucester stretch of the Mall, is the first sculpture on Commonwealth Avenue to celebrate women's accomplishments. Beginning in 1993, representatives from City Hall, the Boston Women's Commission, the Neighborhood Association of the Back Bay, the Boston Women's Heritage Trail, and other interested parties met, processed, planned, raised funds, and consciousness-raised for this project. Finally, in October 2003, the **Boston Women's Memorial** was dedicated. The women selected for the monument were three Boston writers who had progressive ideas and

Boston Women's Memorial, Commonwealth Avenue Mall

It was a great mistake, my being born a man,
I would have been much more successful as a sea gull or a fish.

—EUGENE O'NEILL, *LONG DAY'S JOURNEY INTO NIGHT* (1941)

a commitment to social change—slave-poet **Phillis Wheatley** (1753–1784), feminist editor **Lucy Stone** (1818–1893), and revolutionary-era scribe, **Abigail Adams** (1744–1818). Like the women depicted, sculptor Meredith Bergmann broke from eighteenth- and nineteenth-century tradition by making the memorial engaging and interactive, and placing the women in and around—rather than *on*—their respective pedestals. Under the guidance of the Boston Women's Heritage Trail, a school curriculum has been developed based on the lives and works of these three writers.

One nearby site, within several long blocks of the Literary Trail, is worth a side trip.

If you continue down Beacon Street past Massachusetts Avenue and beyond the Charlesgate interchange, you will find Bay State Road. During the last two years of his life, playwright **Eugene O'Neill** (1888–1953) and his wife, former actress **Carlotta Monterey** (1888–1970), lived at the Hotel Shelton at 91 Bay State Road. The winner of three Pulitzers and one Nobel Prize, O'Neill was a giant of twentieth-century American theater. His dozens of internationally acclaimed plays include *Beyond the Horizon* (1920), *Anna Christie* (1921), *Desire Under the Elms* (1924), *Strange Interlude* (1928), *Mourning Becomes Electra* (1931), *The Iceman Cometh* (1946), and *Long Day's Journey into Night* (written 1941, posthumously published 1956).

After studying playwriting in George Pierce Baker's 47 Workshop at Harvard, O'Neill founded the Provincetown Players, which first produced his work in 1916 on a rustic Cape Cod wharf. He soon gained the attention of the New York theater community, and a prolific period of writing followed. More than a decade later, O'Neill enjoyed the dubious honor of being "banned in Boston." In 1928, his long and experimental *Strange Interlude* was not allowed to play on Boston stages—though it proved a sellout in nearby Quincy. According to legend, many theatergoers took their intermission break

Eugene and Carlotta O'Neill

at a fast-food operation run by local entrepreneur Howard Johnson, thereby boosting his business into profit and prominence.

Over his lifetime, O'Neill lived in a variety of places, including New York, France, and Marblehead, Massachusetts. During his last years he suffered from a progressive tremor and Parkinson's disease, making writing almost impossible. To be near his doctors in Boston, the O'Neills lived in Suite 401 in the Hotel Shelton, now a Boston University dormitory.

If you are still on the main route of the Literary Trail, follow Commonwealth Avenue from the Boston Women's Memorial past the intersection with Gloucester Street. Stop at the corner of Comm. Ave. and Hereford Street, the last of the alphabet streets in the grid. On the left, 40 Hereford was the home of "the Mother of Level Measurements," the internationally adored author of *The Boston Cooking-School Cook Book*, **Fannie Farmer** (1857–1915).

Born in Boston and raised in nearby Medford, Fannie Merritt Farmer began her cooking career in part because of a disability. Partially paralyzed at seventeen by either a stroke or a polio-like illness, she found herself unable to attend school or socialize. Confined to her home, she found solace and excitement in cooking, first for her family, and later for the boarders the Farmers took in. By the age of thirty, Farmer's culinary talents were so obvious that she was encouraged to enter the reputable Boston Cooking School, at 174 Tremont Street. In the next four years, the graduate became assistant principal, then principal, of the school.

Next, of course, came the book. First published in 1896, the *Boston Cooking-School Cook Book* came to be known worldwide as simply *Fannie Farmer*. When Farmer first took the manuscript to Little, Brown, however, the prestigious house was dubious about its merits. When it turned her down, she agreed to pay for the printing of the first three thousand copies personally. A century and well over 3 million copies later, the book, thoroughly revised, is still a staple of kitchens everywhere.

Farmer's crusade to take the old school of measuring—with a "heaping cup" here and a "rounded teaspoon" there—and bring it into the world of science was revolutionary in the annals of cooking. In this first edition of her book, she warned readers:

> *Correct measurements are absolutely necessary to insure the best results. . . . Good judgment, with experience, has taught some to measure by sight; but the majority need definite guides.*

In 1902 Farmer opened her own establishment, Miss Farmer's School of Cookery, at 30 Huntington Avenue. For a decade beginning in 1905, she also wrote monthly food columns in the *Woman's Home Companion*. Its editors were worried about upsetting her dedicated audience when she died, on January 15, 1915. As a result, they continued to run her columns until the end of the year, never mentioning that their author had passed on.

Proceed down Commonwealth Avenue to Massachusetts Avenue, where you will take a left to the stoplight on Boylston Street, then a right onto Boylston. Two blocks farther on the right, at 1154 Boylston, is the **Massachusetts Historical Society**.

Founded in 1791, the Historical Society first stored its collections of "curiosities" in temporary quarters that included the attic of Faneuil Hall. From 1833 to 1897, it occupied a building at 30 Tremont Street, next to the King's Chapel Burying Ground. It was here that Henry Wadsworth Longfellow read Paul Revere's own manuscript of his famous journey— inspiring the poet to write "Paul Revere's Ride." Published in 1863, in the midst of the Civil War, that poem became a "call to arms," linking one patriotic American war to another.

Fannie Farmer

In 1899, the Historical Society moved to its present home. Today the MHS is the nation's leading research library for the study of American history and collects materials, especially manuscripts, related to the history of the Commonwealth and the nation. Among their varied acquisitions that mark where history and literature intersect are the papers of Ellery Sedgwick, editor of the *Atlantic Monthly* from 1908 to 1938. His correspondents ranged from Carl Sandburg and Virginia Woolf to Felix Frankfurter (on the Sacco and Vanzetti case) and Robert Frost—who was initially rejected by the magazine. The society is a famed repository for the letters and diaries of historical figures from Governor John Winthrop to presidents John and John Quincy Adams. It also holds the papers of romantic nineteenth-century historians George Bancroft, William Hickling Prescott, and Francis Parkman. Henry Adams left his personal papers and library to the society, including the copyright to *The Education of Henry Adams*.

Just beyond the society, where Boylston Street meets the Fenway, is a bust of **John Boyle O'Reilly** (1844–1890), the distinguished Irish-American editor, orator, poet, and crusader for human rights. Sculpted by Daniel Chester French in 1896, the memorial commemorates the editor and co-owner of the powerful Irish-American Catholic newspaper the *Pilot*. A significant link between new Irish immigrants and Boston's old Brahmin culture, O'Reilly was the poet of choice on a variety of historic occasions, including the reunion of the Army of the Potomac and the dedication of Plymouth Rock.

Mary Baker Eddy

Retrace your steps on Boylston to the intersection with Massachusetts Avenue. Take a right on Mass. Ave., and follow it toward Huntington Avenue, where you'll find an architecturally impressive plaza of buildings, arches, gardens, and courtyards, mirrored in a reflecting pool. The new **Mary Baker Eddy Library for the Betterment of Humanity**, at 200 Massachusetts Avenue, includes a variety of chambers and halls—some public, some paid exhibits, and some

> *We are all sculptors, working at various forms,*
> *moulding and chiseling thought.*
>
> —MARY BAKER EDDY, *SCIENCE AND HEALTH* (1875)

---

closed to the public—including a library, library shop, and reference and research rooms, as well as the famed Mapparium, the Hall of Ideas, the Quest Gallery, and the "Quotes" Café. It is also the home of the Pulitzer Prize–winning newspaper, the *Christian Science Monitor*, founded in 1908.

All of this is the legacy of **Mary Baker Eddy** (1821-1910), the pathfinding nineteenth-century publisher, author, teacher, public speaker, and founder of the first Church of Christ, Scientist (chartered in Boston in 1879). Born and raised in rural New Hampshire, plagued by ill health in her childhood and early adulthood, and widowed in her twenties, Mary Morse Baker was in constant search of cures. At a time when medicine was an all-male profession and medical practices harsh and primitive, she began seeking alternative therapies, eventually moving toward those that combined mind/body connections with her own spiritual journey. The prayer-based system of healing she developed—mind–body–spirit—not only brought her health, but was found to be replicable and teachable. She named it "Christian Science" and founded a medical college to teach it.

Eddy was not only fighting the entrenched, male-dominated medical establishment, but the entrenched, male-dominated religious establishment as well. In the exhibits and literature now readily available through the new research library—opened in 2002 following a two-year, $50 million building project—visitors can discover how Eddy (she married her third husband, Asa Gilbert Eddy, in 1877) was a pioneer both in the realm of spiritualism and mind/body healing and in the early movement for women's rights and women's emergence into the public sphere.

Eddy's major published work, initially released in 1875 as *Science and Health* (later known as *Science and Health with Key to the Scriptures*) sold fewer than six hundred copies in its first year. That book, however, became the textbook for teaching and practicing Christian Science and proved to be a perennial bestseller: more than 10 million copies have been sold in seventeen languages and English Braille. Meanwhile, she wrote numerous other books and public addresses, published and edited a monthly magazine, founded a church and a college, and created the Christian Science Publishing Society.

When Eddy was in her senior years, her son, George—fearing he would not inherit her fortune—tried to run her affairs and have her declared incompetent, a suit financed by media mogul Joseph Pulitzer. Forced out of retirement by the sensational newspaper coverage that followed and required to defend her sanity in an interview with a court-appointed psychiatrist, Eddy founded the *Christian Science Monitor*—at the age of 87! Initially created as an ethical alternative to the yellow journalism rampant at the turn of the twentieth century, the *Monitor* is still considered an international newspaper of exceptional merit, balance, and journalistic integrity. (The court, by the way, dismissed the lawsuit.)

Take a left at the reflecting pool of the Christian Science Plaza, then follow Huntington Avenue back to **Copley Square**. The former "Art Square"—renamed in 1883 to honor artist John Singleton Copley—holds two of Boston's architectural masterpieces: Trinity Church and the McKim Building of the Boston Public Library.

For centuries, libraries were the private domains of the learned, moneyed few. Even by the middle of the nineteenth century, the area's two largest book repositories were the private Boston Athenaeum and the Harvard College Library, accessible only to faculty and students. By 1854, however, literacy became the right of Everyman when the **Boston Public Library** opened its doors on Mason Street, near the Common, to become the country's first major free municipal library. The mass of immigrants who lived in the city by mid-century—and the Yankees' desire to educate and acculturate them—was a major incentive for creating both public libraries and public schools.

By 1895, the Boston Public Library had found a third, permanent home in Copley Square in a stunning structure designed by Charles Follen McKim and inspired by the Italian Renaissance. Entering the building from Dartmouth Street, you'll immediately notice three huge bronze doors in the vestibule, depicting Music and Poetry, Knowledge and Wisdom, and Truth and Romance, designed by Daniel Chester French. Some of the finest artists of the time—including French, Louis and Augustus Saint-Gaudens, John Singer

*All persons using the Library must conduct themselves
in such a manner as not to interfere with or cause annoyance
to others; and to this end all annoying and disagreeable behavior,
such as hawking, spitting on the floor, humming, whistling,
whispering is strictly prohibited.*

—RULES AND REGULATIONS OF THE PUBLIC LIBRARY OF THE CITY OF BOSTON,
REVISED MARCH 1896

Sargent, Puvis de Chavannes, and Edwin Austin Abbey—were called on to create decorative pieces for the library, both inside and out.

Once inside, you'll be in an ornate lobby of Roman design. Embedded in the mosaic domes above are the names of famous Bostonians, grouped into categories such as theologians, artists, reformers, and historians. The literary figures so commemorated include Hawthorne, Emerson, Longfellow, but—a testament to the times—not a single female. Ascend the main staircase, which Henry James loved for "its amplitude of wing and its splendour of tawny marble, a high and luxurious beauty."

At the top of the staircase is the building's centerpiece, the majestic, 218-foot-long Bates Hall. It was named for wealthy financier Joshua Bates—a senior partner in Baring Brothers, the London banking firm—who had long dreamed of creating a grand reading room that would be open to the public without charge. As a poor boy growing up on the South Shore, Bates taught himself to read in the back rooms of Boston's bookstores. Bates's donation of $100,000 as well as some 30,000 books made him a major benefactor of the new library building.

On its opening, Bates Hall was compared to "the hall of a great Roman bath, with decorative elements of the Italian Renaissance superimposed." The reviewer for the Boston *Daily Globe* found himself almost speechless in his report of February 1, 1895:

> *Boston's new public library is done. It is the finest library building in the world, and contains the second largest collection of books and pamphlets in the United States. . . . Bates Hall is the apartment that has baffled all descriptive writers. It is so grand, so immense, and so noble in conception and effect, that it is beyond the limitation of words.*

One of the dreams behind the creation of public libraries—to serve and integrate the immigrant population—was certainly fulfilled in Boston. A shining example is **Mary Antin** (1881–1949), who fled from Russian Poland's czarist regime in 1894 and emigrated to the United States. The unschooled but ambitious peasant took every opportunity she could to improve her mind and her life in the land of the free. She attended public school in Boston, published poems in local newspapers as a child, and wrote *From Plotzk to Boston*—a chronicle of life in the Jewish Pale and her family's emigration—while still a youth. Among her many admirers was Edward Everett Hale, who gave her free run of his personal book collection.

In her autobiography, *The Promised Land* (1912), Antin applauded that other masterful book collection—the Boston Public Library—as "a noble treasure house of learning":

Public Library—Built by the People—Free to All. Did I not say it was my palace? Mine, because I was a citizen; mine, though I was born an alien; mine, though I lived on Dover Street. My palace—mine!

Kahlil Gibran, circa 1910

The library was just as beloved by great writers and scholars as by ordinary folk. The Alcott family, Ralph Waldo Emerson, Oliver Wendell Holmes, John Greenleaf Whittier, Lucy Larcom, Henry Wadsworth Longfellow, Sarah Orne Jewett, John Boyle O'Reilly, and Nathaniel Hawthorne were among those who worked here.

Today the Boston Public Library remains a treasured gem, serving all the citizens of Massachusetts. It is one of only two public libraries qualified to belong to the Association of Research Libraries. The McKim Building has been declared a National Historic Landmark. Regular guided tours offer visitors an informed view of the institution, past and present, including its wealth of fine art and architecture.

You pray in your distress and in your need;
would that you might pray also in the fullness of
your joy and in your days of abundance.

—KAHLIL GIBRAN, *THE PROPHET* (1923)

While in Copley Square, stop at the **Kahlil Gibran Monument**, across the street and directly facing the McKim Building.

Kahlil Gibran (1883–1931) was a first-generation Lebanese immigrant who lived and worked on Tyler Street, in Boston's Chinatown, where he wrote his most famous book, *The Prophet* (1923). A poet, philosopher, and artist, he was considered the genius of his age by Arabic-speaking people, and has remained a source of spiritual insight and inspiration to all nationalities since his death. This memorial, a bronze bas-relief of the young poet on a pink granite slab, was sculpted by Kahlil Gibran, his godson, cousin, co-biographer, and namesake. It is inscribed with the poet's acknowledgment of the aid given him by Boston and its Brahmins: "It was in my heart to help a little because I was helped much."

When the elder Gibran died in 1931, his body lay in a receiving tomb at Forest Hills Cemetery, in the Jamaica Plain neighborhood of Boston, before being shipped to Lebanon for interment.

Forest Hills Cemetery:
A Walking Tour
Approximate Time: 1–3 Hours

Directions: *Forest Hills Cemetery is located at 95 Forest Hills Avenue in Jamaica Plain. From Park Drive or Brookline Avenue, take the winding Jamaicaway to the Arnold Arboretum. Continue around the rotary onto Route 203 East, past the Arboretum's main entrance, then go one more mile, crossing the Casey overpass, to the Forest Hills rotary. The entrance to the cemetery is just beyond, at the junction of Morton Street (203 E) and Forest Hills Avenue. By public transportation, the cemetery is a short walk from the Forest Hills MBTA stop, on the Orange Line.*

The Puritans who settled New England warned of frightening scenarios of fiery afterlife in their sermons, and disposed of their dead accordingly. Colonial Boston's graveyards became bleak repositories that reflected the harsh realities of life and a hellfire-and-damnation view of death. Grave-stones were often stark slate markers, simply carved with names and dates or decorated with symbols like a skull and crossbones, the Grim Reaper, an hourglass, or a winged death's head. Gravesites were used again and again, with family, friends, and strangers piling one upon another, some-times five and six deep.

By the early nineteenth century, these burying grounds were often over-crowded with bodies, overgrown with weeds, and generally decrepit. They were also assumed to be the source of noxious odors and contagious disease. More than a century earlier, writers such as John Milton and Alexander Pope had observed that properly "shaped" land was capable of evoking nostalgia and profound emotion. In the meantime, new, romantic attitudes about death and afterlife had come into fashion. Rather than focusing on eternal damnation like their colonial ancestors, many began to see death as an ethereal repose. Hence, burying grounds that were more attuned to nature, and more conducive to calm and eternal rest, began to emerge. Following the model of English pleasure parks and Père Lachaise Cemetery in Paris (1804), Americans embarked on a new era of burial practice. The church graveyard gave way to the "cemetery," the French *cimitière*, from the Greek term for a place of rest.

In 1831, the first rural garden cemetery in America, Mount Auburn, was dedicated in Cambridge, Massachusetts. Seventeen years later, Forest

Hills—in historic Roxbury, now the Jamaica Plain neighborhood of Boston—was consecrated as a city cemetery. Though Mount Auburn was private and Forest Hills originally municipal (the latter was privatized after two decades), they shared a similar design and vision: beautifully carved memorials, often by famous sculptors, were scattered over naturally landscaped hills and dales, laced with winding paths, wistful trees and plantings, and reflecting pools. Poignant, often literary, inscriptions were carved on their intricately designed stones. Both cemeteries, as a result, attracted creative, nature-loving people who wished to spend eternity in a quiet and artful rural setting.

At the main gate of **Forest Hills,** pick up a large street map to guide you through the 280-acre cemetery and help you find individual memorials. You can purchase a comprehensive book and self-guided walking tour, *Garden of Memories: A Guide to Historic Forest Hills* (by Susan Wilson, 1998) at the front office. Check at that office or on the Forest Hills Educational Trust Web site for information on guided walking tours, special arts events, and lectures.

Though people from all social classes, races, religions, and professions have chosen Forest Hills as their last destination, there are a great number of authors, playwrights, poets, journalists, and historians. Among those buried here (and described in detail elsewhere on the Literary Trail) are playwright **Eugene O'Neill,** poets **E. E. Cummings** and **Anne Sexton,** writers **Edward Everett Hale, Susanna Haswell Rowson,** and **George Ticknor,** and abolitonists **William Lloyd Garrison** and **William Cooper Nell.**

Here is found some of the finest statuary work of **Daniel Chester French.** Directly beyond the main gate, you can see his funerary masterpiece, *Death and the Sculptor*, a high-relief bronze tribute to his fellow artists **Martin** and **Joseph Milmore.** Curiously, the sculptor depicted in this work is carving a Sphinx, a direct reference to the Civil War memorial that Martin Milmore created for Mount Auburn Cemetery (and that faces Bigelow Chapel to this day). Other sculptures by French at Forest Hills include a winged tribute to one of Boston's major benefactors, George Robert White (who is also memorialized by a statue in the Public Garden). Indeed, Forest Hills Cemetery has one of the finest collections of Victorian memorial sculpture in the nation.

A variety of literary figures not yet encountered on the Literary Trail are also interred at Forest Hills. Among them are writers **Nancy Hale Bowers** (*The Young Die Good*) and **Frederick Lewis Allen** (*Only Yesterday*), historians **Annie Haven Thwing** (*The Crooked and Narrow Streets of Boston*) and **Samuel Gardner Drake** (*Indian Biographies*), diarist **Anna Cabot Lowell** (*Journal of My Conduct*), and composer **Amy**

Marcy Cheney Beach, the first American woman to write symphonies, which were performed by prestigious organizations like the Handel and Haydn Society, the Boston Symphony Orchestera, and the New York Symphony Orchestra.

Charles H. Taylor, the first member of the *Boston Globe* dynasty, is buried here, as is the radical German-American newspaper editor **Karl Heinzen** (*Pionier*). **John Sullivan Dwight,** the acclaimed nineteenth-century music critic and literary reviewer (*Dwight's Journal of Music*), **Oliver Ditson**, America's most successful nineteenth-century music publisher, and **Curtis Guild, Sr.,** the writer, drama critic, and newspaperman who founded *Boston's Commercial Bulletin*, one of the most important business journals of its day, can also be found here. Interred at Forest Hills as well is **Clarence Walker Barron,** the father of modern financial analysis and an owner of the *Wall Street Journal. Barron's* magazine still bears his name.

Bookbinder **Herbert Mosely Plimpton** is also a resident of Forest Hills. He was the founder of the Plimpton Press, long the largest book bindery in New England. Plimpton Press helped pioneer "one-stop-shopping" in the book industry—moving a book through the complete process from manuscript to bound volume in a single plant.

Among the many interesting tales in the annals of Forest Hills are these two, concerning **Eugene O'Neill** and **E. E. Cummings:**

When O'Neill died in the Hotel Shelton on November 27, 1953, he had already created his obituary notice: "Born in a goddam hotel room and dying in a hotel room!" To avoid the public and the press, his wife asked J. S. Waterman & Sons Funeral Home to whisk her husband away quietly to Forest Hills—no fanfare, flash bulbs, or elaborate funeral. Though fans stole flowers and other tokens from the gravesite for years thereafter, today they tend to leave gifts instead: a small cairn, or memorial rock pile, is often found on O'Neill's headstone, in the area known as Sleepy Hollow.

After Cummings died of a cerebral hemorrhage on September 3, 1962, he was buried in Forest Hills in the lot of the Clarkes—his mother's side of the family. Ironically, the man associated with calculated disregard for uppercase letters was memorialized with a simple flush marker that reads EDWARD ESTLIN CUMMINGS in bold capitals. One of his most telling observations on death can be found in his poem "Since Feeling Is First":

for life's not
a paragraph and
death I think
is no parenthesis.

The Literary Trail now moves on to Cambridge, a trip best executed by car or on a tour bus. If you are leaving the Boston Public Library by car, head west on the Massachusetts Turnpike from Copley Square.

Driving on the Mass. Pike, you'll soon see the floodlights of Fenway Park hovering on your left. Fabulous Fenway—the home of the Boston Red Sox since 1912—has inspired countless literary musings. Among the classics is **John Updike**'s "Hub Fans Bid Kid Adieu," written after seeing Ted Williams play his last game on September 28, 1960:

Our noise for some seconds passed beyond excitement into a kind of immense open anguish, a cry to be saved. But immortality is not transferable. The papers said that the other players, and even the umpires on the field, begged him to come out and acknowledge us in some way, but he never had and did not now. Gods do not answer letters.

In 1999 the master of the macabre, **Stephen King** (b. 1947), used a Red Sox relief hitter as the inspiration for his best-selling novel *The Girl Who Loved Tom Gordon*. The popular writer has also been a prolific one, writing new horror and science fiction novels almost every year for some time. In the wake of Boston's victory in the 2004 World Series, King and Stewart O'Nan wrote *Faithful: Two Diehard Boston Red Sox Fans Chronicle the Historic 2004 Season*, one of literally hundreds of books inspired by that spectacular win. Among the many fine books written about Fenway, its history, and its colorful characters, incidentally, is the lavishly illustrated *Red Sox Century* (2000), by sports historians Glen Stout and Richard Johnson.

Leave the Mass. Pike at the Cambridge/Allston exit, staying to the right. Continue straight over the bridge across the Charles River. The river, of course, has inspired many writers throughout Boston's history, including Annie Adams Fields:

[Before the embankments were added, the Charles River] was wider and more beautiful. Early in the morning, sometimes before sunrise, standing at my bedroom window I have seen [Oliver Wendell Holmes's] tiny skiff moving quickly over the face of the quiet water. Sometimes the waves were high and rough. . . . There was little to be learned about a skiff and its management which he did not acquire.

*I have just returned from Boston.
It is the only sane thing to do if you
find yourself up there.*

—FRED ALLEN, LETTER TO GROUCHO MARX (1953)

Once over the Charles, take a left onto Memorial Drive. The well-maintained Riverside Press Park, immediately on your right, is the site of the **Riverside Press**, an important chapter in Boston's publishing history. In 1846, a twenty-three-year-old Vermonter named Henry O. Houghton moved to Cambridge and set up his printing shop near Harvard. When his business outgrew the modest space, he moved his firm to the banks of the Charles—to a building on River Street that had been built as an almshouse for the city in 1838. Little, Brown and Company had purchased the building earlier that year and converted it to a printing plant.

Houghton's Riverside Press served many prestigious publishing houses such as Little, Brown, G. C. Merriam, and Ticknor & Fields—also printing the latter's popular magazine, the *Atlantic Monthly*. Meanwhile, as William Ticknor and James T. Fields and their Old Corner Bookstore grew, so too did Henry Houghton and his printing plant. Fields became the sole proprietor of his firm after Ticknor's death in 1864. Houghton took on George Harrison Mifflin as a partner in 1872.

By 1880, the Boston publisher and Cambridge printer merged, creating Houghton, Mifflin and Company. The Riverside Press was maintained as a subsidiary until 1966 and the Ticknor & Fields imprint restored as a tribute to the old company, from 1979 to 1992. The facility on this site was closed by Houghton Mifflin in 1971 and the building demolished two years later. A coalition of city and neighborhood workers created and dedicated the namesake Riverside Press Park in 1981.

Follow Memorial Drive, with the river on your left, until you turn right into Harvard Square on John F. Kennedy Street. Driving toward the Square, you'll pass Harvard's John F. Kennedy Park and the **John F. Kennedy School of Government** on your left. Countless great names in government, politics, public affairs, and history have taught, lectured, attended classes, or otherwise passed through its doors, including Marvin Kalb (*Kissinger*), Graham Allison (*Essence of Decision*), and Richard Neustadt and Ernest May (*The Uses of History*).

Glance to the left as you pass Eliot Street. Behind the Kennedy School you can see the elegant Charles Hotel complex, which includes a fitness center long frequented by **Robert B. Parker** (b. 1932). Like his fictional gumshoe, the man known simply as Spenser, Parker is famous for keeping in shape. The very literate and likable Spenser, meanwhile, has appeared in more than two dozen novels. His character has was spun off into a popular 1980s TV series (*Spenser for Hire*) and a run of movies for cable TV.

Another place that Robert Parker has often been seen and heard over the past two decades is in an unusual local bookstore of international fame. Though not on the route of the Literary Trail, **Kate's Mystery Books**—located less than two miles from Harvard Square, down Massachusetts Avenue toward Arlington—is definitely worth a visit, either in person or via their Web site, www.katesmytserybooks.com. Owner Kate Mattes opened her shop in a Victorian house at 2211 Mass. Ave. on Friday the 13th in May 1983. Over the years, her quirky store has become the hub for things mysterious, suspenseful, and, of course, literary. Late in 2004, Mattes moved into book publishing as well, founding the Kate's Mystery Books imprint in partnership with Justin, Charles & Company, a new Boston publisher.

2

{CAMBRIDGE}

The histories of Boston and Cambridge have so intertwined over the centuries that many people assume they are two parts of a single city. Both towns played major roles in the crises, cries, and conflicts that snowballed into the American Revolution by 1775. And both have proved pivotal in the development of American literary and cultural life from colonial times through the present day.

Harvard Yard, 1871 (see page 118)

The initial settlement of these two towns was, in fact, only a few months apart. During the summer of 1630, Charlestown, Boston, Roxbury, and Watertown were all founded by members of the Massachusetts Bay Company. Perceiving the need for a fortified town to function as a capital, the governor and his assistants founded "Newtowne" (the original name for Cambridge) on December 28, 1630. In 1634, Boston was made the seat of government, and in 1636 the General Court selected Newtowne over Salem as the location for the colony's first college.

When Harvard College was founded in 1636—the first institution of higher learning in Britain's North American colonies—it established Cambridge as an intellectual center. As a result, Cambridge boasted the first printing press in the colonies (1638) and swiftly became a magnet for writers, educators, and academicians. By the nineteenth and twentieth centuries, this group included many of the leading literary figures in the country, from Henry James, Alice James, Henry

Wadsworth Longfellow, Margaret Fuller, Robert Frost, and Eugene O'Neill to E. E. Cummings, Gertrude Stein, Vladimir Nabokov, May Sarton, Helen Vendler, Cornel West, and Henry Louis Gates, Jr.

William Dean Howells, himself a writer and editor, made note of the extraordinary bounty of Cambridge-based literati in *Literary Friends and Acquaintance* (1900):

> *The variety of talents and achievements was indeed so great that Mr. Bret Harte . . . justly said . . . "Why, you couldn't fire a revolver from your front porch anywhere [in Cambridge] without bringing down a two-volumer!"*

The reclusive poet Emily Dickinson reacted to this phenomenon with awe and appreciation:

> *[Moving to Cambridge is] like moving to Westminster Abbey, as hallowed and as unbelieved, or moving to Ephesus with Paul for a next-door neighbor.*

The two areas of Cambridge most closely associated with the Golden Age of American Literature are the **Harvard University** campus—flowing in and out of Harvard Yard and Harvard Square—and **Brattle Street**.

After following John F. Kennedy Street from the Charles River to Harvard Square, pause at the center of the Square. To the right is a pedestrian mall, where you'll see an entrance to the "T," a Bostix ticket booth, and the famed Out of Town news stand. In 1631, **Anne Bradstreet** (ca. 1612–1672), the colonies' first female poet, made her home on this site, facing today's Harvard Yard.

The daughter of Thomas Dudley, an early governor of the Massachusetts Bay Colony, Anne married Simon Bradstreet at the age of sixteen and arrived in America on the ship *Arbella* in 1630. In the

*It is a true error to marry
with poets
or to be by them.*

—JOHN BERRYMAN, *77 DREAM SONGS* (1964)

---

early days of the Puritan settlement, literature rarely strayed from religious sermons and personal journals. Despite the restrictive atmosphere—and the time and energy it took to raise eight children while supporting her husband's political ambitions—Anne wrote poems, prose "meditations," and letters, publishing more than four hundred pages of verse during her lifetime.

Though some consider her poetry unoriginal, Shaun O'Connell noted in *Imagining Boston* that "Bradstreet's spiritual autobiography helped define a literary mode which would persist, with telling variations and revisions, for three centuries." In 1964, poet **John Berryman** (1914–1972) wrote the lengthy *Homage to Mistress Bradstreet*, who proved an inspiration to him three centuries after her death. Berryman, like Bradstreet, once lived in Harvard Square. Today, Harvard's Houghton Library, on the opposite side of Harvard Yard from the spot where the poet lived, maintains Bradstreet's original manuscripts.

Harvard Square: A Walking Tour
Approximate Time: 90 Minutes

Harvard Square, often called simply "the Square," was named for its proximity to the Harvard College campus. Though there are other bustling, commercial "squares" in Cambridge—notably Central, Kendall, Inman, and Porter—Harvard Square has asserted its dominance in things cultural for close to four centuries.

Begin this walking trip at the site of poet **Anne Bradstreet**'s home, near the Out of Town newsstand. As you walk up Mass. Ave. past the Cambridge Savings Bank, you'll see Dunster Street, parallel to JFK Street, on your right. Around the corner of Dunster and up one story on the brick façade is a plaque honoring Stephen Day, who lived on this site. Day established **America's first printing press** nearby in 1638 and ran it under the auspices of the infant college. Among his early printing projects was the *Bay Psalm Book,* the colonies' first collection of metrical versions of the Psalms, which became more popular than any other English psalter. Though seventeen hundred copies of the book were printed in 1640, fewer than a dozen survive. The *Bay Psalm Book* had three prestigious editors: the Reverend Richard Mather, the first of the line of Mathers to settle in the New World; the Reverend John Eliot, the famed "Apostle to the Indians"; and the Reverend Thomas Weld, an ancestor of the governor of Massachusetts some three and a half centuries later. (William Weld was an author himself; after leaving office in 1997, he turned to writing mysteries, beginning with *Mackerel by Moonlight.*)

One block farther, the corner of Mass. Ave. and Holyoke Street once held the University Book Store, run by the prodigious reader and entrepreneur **John Bartlett** (1820–1905). A local legend for his ability to recall or quickly locate the sources of quotations, Bartlett published his first volume of *Familiar Quotations* in 1855.

Because of its extensive literary history, academic appeal, and large student population, the city has always had a wide and diverse array of bookshops. Depending on the month and year, Cambridge generally boasts from two to three dozen bookstores, two-thirds of which are in Harvard Square. (The exact statistics are also subject to your definition of "bookstore" and

Justin Kaplan on John Bartlett and his *Familiar Quotations*

One of the books I brought with me when I came to Harvard as a freshman in 1941 was an edition of *Bartlett's Familiar Quotations*. I hadn't realized then that my room at Apley Court was just around the corner from the site of the bookstore Bartlett owned before the Civil War, that he lived on Brattle Street, a short distance from his friends Henry Wadsworth Longfellow and James Russell Lowell, and that he's buried in nearby Mount Auburn Cemetery, the nation's first and probably most beautiful "park of repose." Many decades later I was privileged to succeed (in a limited sense) Bartlett as editor of *Familiar Quotations*. Over the century and a half since its first edition came out this wonderful old warhorse of a reference book has been regularly updated and enlarged in order to shuck off the time-worn and irrelevant, take in the fresh and timely, and cast a wider net.

Born in 1820, John Bartlett lived to see his name become as generic for quotations as Noah Webster's for definitions. He read widely, kept notes on his reading, and made himself an information bank for members of the local history and academic community. They turned to Bartlett when they wanted to know who said what, when, and where. In 1855 he brought out his first collection of "phrases and familiar quotations which have become 'household words.'" By the time he died in 1905 he had brought out nine editions in all.

A remarkably energetic man, Bartlett had many interests other than quotations. He was an acknowledged authority on fishing, chess, and whist, and estimated he had spent sixteen thousand hours compiling, with the help of his wife, Hannah, a concordance to Shakespeare.

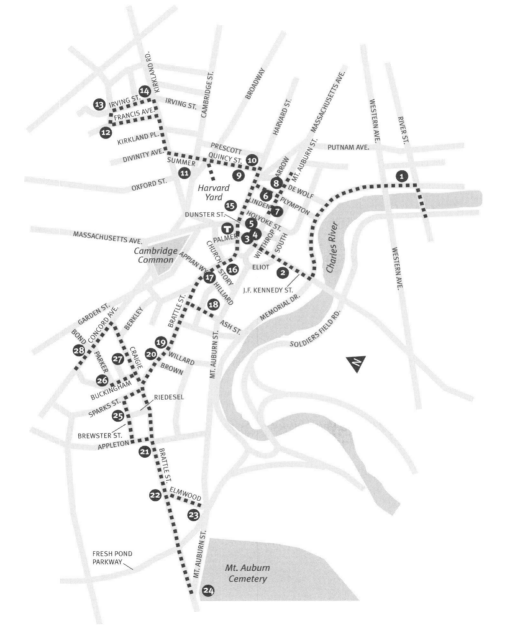

your definition of "Harvard Square.") No matter what the numbers, it's indisputable that the head count—the number of booksellers per capita—is unusually high for any American city or town. Meanwhile, the **Out of Town news stand** at the center of Harvard Square continues to stock newspapers and journals from around the world.

Two blocks beyond Holyoke Street on Mass. Ave. is Plympton Street. The venerable **Grolier Poetry Book Shop**, at 6 Plympton, has been an important gathering and performance space for writers and poets since 1927. The store has been revered and inhabited by four generations of poets and their friends, garnering such accolades as *Boston Magazine*'s Best-of-Boston Award ("Best Poetry Store and Readings") to this day.

Next door, 8 Plympton was once the home of **Conrad Aiken** (1889–1973), a novelist, critic, anthologist, and Pulitzer Prize–winning poet. Aiken moved here in 1915 to be near his mentor, John Gould Fletcher. Meanwhile, in 1929, British novelist **Malcolm Lowry** (1909–1957) came to work with Aiken as an apprentice.

Just beyond, at number 14, is the home of the **Harvard *Crimson***, the spawning ground of many great writers and journalists. **Richard Wilbur** (b. 1921), a prize-winning poet and translator, lived at 22 Plympton while working on his master's degree at Harvard after World War II. Like so many other Harvard grads, Wilbur went on to teach at Harvard and other institutions.

The oddly shaped, colorful building where Plympton meets Bow Street, at 44 Bow, belongs to the ***Harvard Lampoon***. Founded in 1876, it is the world's oldest continuously published humor magazine. An inordinate number of *Lampoon* alumni have become Hollywood scriptwriters and include some of America's finest literary talent. John Updike, George Plimpton, William Gaddis, George Santayana, and publisher William Randolph Hearst—who gave the magazine its building—were all 'Poonies. Robert Benchley, who edited the *Lampoon* with Frederick Lewis Allen (*Only Yesterday*) in the 1920s, made the ultimate observation about pens, popularity, and self-knowledge:

> *It took me fifteen years to discover that I had no talent for writing, but I couldn't give it up because by that time I was too famous.*

Standing by the *Lampoon*, look toward the river to see a tall white spire topped by an ornate weathervane dominating the skyline. This is Lowell

House, one of Harvard's undergraduate residence halls, where the Pulitzer Prize–winner
John Updike (b.1932) spent his college years.
Known best for his novels *Rabbit Run*, *Rabbit
Redux*, *Couples*, and *The Witches of Eastwick*,
Updike has written more than forty books,
including novels, short stories, poetry, and
criticism, and is the only living author to have
twice won the Pulitzer Prize for fiction. Well
aware of the Boston area's literary heritage,
he based one trilogy—*Roger's Version*, *A Month
of Sundays*, and *S.*—on Hawthorne's *Scarlet
Letter*. Updike chose Ipswich, on the North
Shore, as his permanent home.

John Updike

A stone's throw from the intersection of Plympton and Mount Auburn,
at 47 Mount Auburn Street, was the original **Club 47**, as nurturing a space
for musicians of the Great Folk Revival of the 1960s as the Grolier was for
poets. From 1958 to 1968, Club 47 was the stomping grounds of influential
and internationally known folksingers, poets, and singer-songwriters like
Joan Baez, Bob Dylan, Eric Von Schmidt, Tom Rush, Richard Fariña, Judy
Collins, and the Charles River Valley Boys. By far the best book on the folk
scene of the 1960s is Eric Von Schmidt and Jim Rooney's *Baby Let Me
Follow You Down: The Illustrated Story of the Cambridge Folk Years* (1979).

(This performance venue—now called **Club Passim** and located at 47
Palmer Street, just off Church Street in Harvard Square—remains a haven for
that literary-musical tradition to this day. The inimitable Bob Donlin, who ran
Passim with his wife, Rae Anne, from 1969 through 1995, was one of Jack
Kerouac's "dharma bums," loosely disguised as Bob Donnelly in Kerouac's
novels. Meanwhile, the club has helped to introduce a whole new generation
of talents, musical and literary, including Suzanne Vega, Shawn Colvin, Nanci
Griffith, Bill Morrissey, Patty Larkin, Tracy Chapman, and Ellis Paul.)

Return on Plympton to Mass. Ave. Cross the street, turning right on
Mass. Ave., then left onto Quincy Street. Entering Harvard Yard through the
first gate on your left, you'll be walking directly toward the **Houghton
Library,** which contains manuscripts and rare books belonging to the
Harvard College Library. Opened in 1942, Houghton is an international

Believe in life!
Always human beings will live and
progress to greater, broader, and fuller life.
—W. E. B. DU BOIS, *LAST MESSAGE TO THE WORLD* (1963)

The Houghton Library

W. E. B. Du Bois

resource of exceptional depth and diversity, offering scholars direct access to a wealth of primary sources. The collections, which focus on the study of Western civilization, include the working papers of living novelists and poets as well as the personal effects, notes, books, and other objects of interest from writers such as Copernicus, Emily Dickinson, John Keats, Edward Lear, Dante, Tennessee Williams, Goethe, Cervantes, and Lewis Carroll.

Directly across the street from Houghton, in the Barker Center at 12 Quincy Street, is the **W. E. B. Du Bois Institute** of Harvard University, named for **William Edward Burghardt Du Bois**, the first African American awarded a Ph.D. from Harvard (1895). Du Bois is often considered the most influential black thinker of the first half of the twentieth century. His many accomplishments range from numerous articles and books, including *The Souls of Black Folk* and *John Brown*, to helping establish the National Association for the Advancement of Colored People (NAACP) in 1909. Du Bois lived several blocks away, on Flagg Street.

Continuing down Quincy Street, on the right you will see gateposts numbered 16 and 20. **Richard Henry Dana, Jr**. (1815–1882), lived at 16 Quincy. Like so many youth of his era—who seemed to suffer unduly from ailments of the eyes and nerves—Dana was the victim of failing eyesight. Abandoning his studies at Harvard in

Henry Louis Gates, Jr., on W. E. B. Du Bois

William Edward Burghardt Du Bois was born in Great Barrington, Massachusetts, in 1869, and died in Accra, Ghana, on the eve of the great protest March on Washington in 1963. In his long life, which stretched from Reconstruction to the modern Civil Rights Movement, he became the leading African American public intellectual, the chief spokesperson for racial equality in America, and the symbol of world-wide Pan-Africanism. Du Bois's Greater Boston connections were strengthened by his study at Harvard University, where he took a B.A. in 1890 and a Ph.D. in history in 1895, the first black American to do so. As an author, Du Bois wrote in every conceivable genre: essays, historical monographs, sociological studies, fiction, biographies, editiorials and news reports, and even three autobiographies. His *The Souls of Black Folk* (1903) is arguably the most important book written by an African American. He is probably best remembered for his prophetic prediction, "The problem of the twentieth century is the problem of the color line."

Du Bois particularly inspired and influenced me with his vision of an accurate and comprehensive encyclopedia on Africa and the lives and cultures of peoples of African descent throughout the world. It has been my privilege to co-edit with K. Anthony Appiah an encyclopedia on CD-ROM entitled *Encarta Africana* which, I believe, fulfills Du Bois's dream to correct historical inaccuracies, to cover materials ignored in standard reference works, and to see the African Diaspora whole. This is the deepest tribute I know how to pay to the memory of a great American fighter for justice, a literary figure of immense significance, and a New Englander of international stature.

*The moral is that the flower of art blooms only where
the soil is deep, that it takes a great deal of history
to produce a little literature, that it needs a complex
machinery to set a writer in motion.*

—HENRY JAMES, *HAWTHORNE* (1879)

1834, he signed up as a sailor on a brig bound for California. Invigorated by his adventures on the sea, as well as by a year working the hide-trading ports of California, Dana returned home with healed spirits and vision. The book for which he is still remembered, *Two Years Before the Mast* (1840), was the result of those travels.

Although the book was an immediate success and helped to win the passage of new laws for the protection of sailors, Dana never produced any volume that popular again. He graduated from Harvard Law School in 1839 and became a prime defender in the Anthony Burns fugitive slave trial. Thereafter, in his own judgment, he failed to live up to his youthful promise.

Number 20 Quincy Street, now the site of the Harvard Faculty Club, was once the home of the James family. Both **Henry James, Jr.** (1843–1916), and his sister, **Alice James** (1848–1892), lived here.

Henry James, Jr., was born in New York City, and—with brothers William, Garth, and Robertson—was given an eclectic, unorthodox education with private tutors and constant access to new books and unusual experiences. From their earliest years, the children accompanied their parents to England, France, Switzerland, and Germany, gathering what their father considered "a better sensuous education than they are likely to get here." Two years after the Jameses returned to America in 1860, Henry entered Harvard Law School.

All his travels and studies ultimately filtered into his adult world of literature and writing. After being "discovered" and befriended by William Dean Howells, James saw his first stories, essays, and criticisms printed in the *Atlantic Monthly*. His writings quickly impressed the New England *literati* as well as English masters like Tennyson and Ruskin. In 1869, James moved to England permanently. Boston, in his opinion, was not a worthy place to live and work, being decidedly short on culture, aesthetics, and inspiration.

Over the next four decades James established himself as one of the greatest American novelists. He also became one of the nation's best-known expatriates. He eventually became a British citizen, explaining, "I have testi-fied to my long attachment here in the only way I could—though I certainly shouldn't have done it . . . if the U.S.A. had done a little more for me." George Bernard Shaw wryly observed that the move was a subtle one: "James felt buried in America; but he came here to be embalmed."

Though his topics and characters varied widely, James frequently wrote about the moral struggles of Americans in their homeland, the plight of Americans abroad, and the difficulties they had moving into European society. Among his many books—several of which have been made into movies—are *The Europeans* (1878), *Hawthorne* (1879), *Daisy Miller* (1879), *Washington Square* (1881), *The Portrait of a Lady* (1881), *The Bostonians* (1886), and *The Wings of the Dove* (1902).

James was not afraid of strong women—nor of late-nineteenth-century feminism—like many of his literary peers. His female protagonists in *Daisy Miller* and *Portrait of a Lady* were often in search of independence. Part of James's view of women came from his fascination with the "Boston marriage" of Sarah Orne Jewett and Annie Fields after the death of James T. Fields in 1881. His acceptance of their partnership helped him understand and honor the same relationship his sister Alice had with Katharine Peabody Loring. These women, as well as feminist Elizabeth Peabody, helped to inspire James's characters in *The Bostonians*.

Being the sister of Henry and William James was not easy for Alice James. Like William, she was often incapacitated by psychosomatic ill-nesses and severe depression. It wasn't until she met Loring, who cared for her as a semi-invalid, that the gifted and enigmatic Alice began to blossom. Her journals, which Henry considered beautiful, eloquent, and filled with independence, became beacons for later generations of femi-nists—including the poetry cooperative that

Henry James

formed Alice James Books in 1973. Originally published as her *Journal* (1894, 1934), Alice James's complete writings later appeared under the title *Diary* (1964). Jean Strouse's *Alice James: A Biography* (1980) is a fine study of her life.

A sense of Alice James's unusual strength of spirit can be seen in this *Diary* entry of November 19, 1889:

> *When will women begin to have the first glimmer that above all other loyalties is the loyalty to Truth, i.e. to yourself, that husbands, children, friends, and country are as nothing to that?*

Memorial Hall

Follow Quincy Street across Broadway and Cambridge Street. Dominating your view on the left is Harvard's **Memorial Hall**, a Ruskinian Gothic structure. Conceived as a living memorial to alumni who served or died in the Civil War, Memorial Hall was also built to house an academic theater for literary festivals and a dining hall large enough for graduation dinners.

At its completion in 1878, Henry James found Memorial Hall a curiously ironic structure, "the great bristling brick Valhalla . . . that house of honor and hospitality which . . . dispenses . . . laurels to the dead and dinners to the living." A century later, mystery writer Jane Langton found it a splendid site for a murder. In *The Memorial Hall Murder* (1978), Homer Kelly investigates the death of a chorus leader in the bowels of the building:

> *The building rose above him like a cliff face, mass piled upon mass, ten thousand of brick laid upon ten thousand. It was ugly, majestically ugly. Augustly, monumentally ugly. It was a red-brick Notre Dame, a bastard Chartres, punctured with stained-glass windows, ribboned around with lofty sentiments in Latin, finialed with metallic crests and pennants, knobbed with the heads of orators. . . . When it had been erected in the 1870s it had been intended as a half-secular, half-sacred memorial to young graduates who had died in the Union cause in the Civil War. Now it was an actual coffin.*

The interior vestibule of Memorial Hall, which separates Sanders Theatre from the huge dining hall, is lined with lofty Latin inscriptions above twenty-eight white marble tablets naming the Civil War dead. In the 1984 film version of James's *The Bostonians*, Christopher Reeve—as the southern Civil War veteran Basil Ransom—stands here, pondering these tablets. There was plenty to ponder: the 136 dead listed on the walls are Union men, while some 64 slain Confederate graduates are never mentioned.

Leaving Memorial Hall, bear right onto Kirkland Street and walk the several blocks to Francis Avenue. Follow Francis to its intersection with Bryant. Here on the left is the **Harvard Divinity School** campus.

Since its founding in 1636, Harvard College—immersed, as it was, in a Puritan stronghold—was closely tied to the Puritan church. Most of the men attending the school in its earliest decades studied religion, though not all went on to become preachers. And though Harvard was indeed expected to provide the British colonies with a learned clergy, the advancement of learning in general, for "the English and Indian Youth of this Country," was the school's broadest purpose, as outlined in its Charter of 1650.

Harvard Divinity School was founded in 1819 and emerged as a hotbed of Unitarianism. Among the many writers and ministers who studied here were Horatio Alger, Jr., Frederic Dan Huntington, Thomas Wentworth Higginson, Francis Greenwood Peabody, and the Reverend Peter J. Gomes.

Unitarian minister **Reverend William Ellery Channing** (1740–1842) was awarded an honorary Doctor of Sacred Theology degree here in 1820. The pastor of Boston's Federal Street Church (1803–1842) and author of several best-selling volumes, Channing influenced New England's greatest transcendentalists—including Emerson, Alcott, James Freeman Clarke, Margaret Fuller, and George Ripley—with his sermons and writings on the divinity of the human soul, moral intution, and the dignity of human nature.

One of the least divine of the Divinity School's graduates was arguably **Horatio Alger, Jr.** (1832–1899). A native of Revere, Massachusetts, from an old Puritan family, Alger was primed for the ministry by his father, a Unitarian clergyman. Graduating from Harvard, he tended to his congregation in Brewster, Massachusetts. Unfortunately, Alger also tended to the choirboys in this small Cape Cod town, and was run out of the church for his untoward behavior.

Alger soon found another career that, perhaps not coincidentally, was also centered on boys. While still in Boston, Alger had agreed to create a boys' book with an uplifting message for publisher and bookseller A. K. Loring, at 319 Washington Street. The happy result was *Frank's Campaign, or What Boys Can Do on the Farm for the Camp*. Moving to New York, Alger became a chaplain and philanthropist for the Newsboys' Lodging House. There he began producing the stream of boys' books that brought him international fame.

The first of the truly successful Horatio Alger stories—tales in which poor boys struggled against adversity and temptation to find success, fame, and wealth—starred Ragged Dick. He was followed by Luck and Pluck, Tattered Tom, and sales in the millions. This phenomenal success led one critic to observe: "Horatio Alger wrote the same novel 135 times and never lost his audience."

On the corner of Bryant and Irving, at 136 Irving Street, is the rear entrance of the **American Academy of Arts and Sciences**. Founded in 1780 during the American Revolution, this scholarly society has always made its headquarters in the Boston area, although it does have other regional centers. In the first decades of the new republic, the members met in the Philosophy Chamber of Harvard College. After sharing quarters with the Boston Athenaeum and later with the Massachusetts Historical Society for many years, the group found a twentieth-century home at 28 Newbury Street. In 1981 it moved to its own building in the beautifully wooded area that was once part of the Shady Hill estate of Charles Eliot Norton, a prominent nineteenth-century art historian at Harvard and editor of the *North American Review* and the *Nation*.

The American Academy's charter stated that its goal was "to cultivate every art and science which may tend to advance the interest, honour, dignity, and happiness of a free, independent and virtuous people." Today, it elects women and men of exceptional achievement to its ranks and conducts projects and studies "responsive to the needs and problems of society." The group also publishes the quarterly journal *Daedalus* and awards an Emerson-Thoreau medal for achievement in literature.

The roster of Academy fellows over the past two centuries is a veritable *Who's Who* of important Americans in science, scholarship, business, public affairs, and the arts. Its literary members over the years include Henry Wadsworth Longfellow, Ralph Waldo Emerson, Daniel Webster, Henry Adams, Henry James, Oliver Wendell Holmes, Samuel Eliot Morison, Willa Cather, May Sarton, and Robert Pinsky.

mr u will not be missed
who as an anthologist
sold the many on the few
not excluding mr u

—E. E. CUMMINGS, *1 X 1* (1944)

Though originally limited to men, the Academy welcomed astronomer and educator **Maria Mitchell** (1818–1889) to its membership in 1848. By the turn of the twenty-first century, almost twenty percent of its 4,000 fellows and 600 Foreign Honorary Members were women. Still, for almost a century, Mitchell was the sole female thus honored.

Follow Irving Street down to Scott and Farrar. Behind the Irving-Scott signpost is a historic marker noting that **E. E. Cummings** (1894–1962) was born here, at 104A Irving. The sign also reminds visitors of one of his most quoted lines, from *Sonnets—Realities* (1923):

the Cambridge ladies who live in furnished souls
are unbeautiful and have comfortable minds.

The son of Rebecca Haswell and Dr. Edward Cummings, the successor to Edward Everett Hale at Boston's Second Congregational Church, the young Edward Estlin Cummings attended Cambridge Latin School and Harvard College (Class of 1915) before joining the French ambulance corps in World War I. An accidental imprisonment in a prisoner-of-war camp gave him material for *The Enormous Room* (1922), his widely acclaimed and only novel.

From there Cummings leapt into America's second great literary renaissance, experimenting with a new, free style of prose and poetry and distinguishing himself as a painter and playwright. The poet became known for not using capital letters—a conceit

E. E. Cummings

> *The union of the mathematician with the poet,*
> *fervor with measure, passion with correctness,*
> *this surely is the ideal.*
>
> —WILLIAM JAMES, *COLLECTED ESSAYS AND REVIEWS* (1920)

---

he explained in several ways. A student of Latin and Greek at Harvard, he observed that classical literature "never began a sentence with a capital." Moreover, he noted, no other language he knew of wrote the first-person singular—the ubiquitous "I"—in capitals.

Contrary to widespread belief (and the popular tendency, both during his lifetime and after, to print his name "e. e. cummings"), Cummings did not have his name legally lower-cased. The poet was also known to both sign and type his own name with upper-case initials.

Throughout his life, Cummings spent considerable time in Paris, Greenwich Village, and his family's rural retreat at Joy Farm, in Silver Lake, New Hampshire. During 1952–53 he was Charles Eliot Norton Professor of Poetry at Harvard, where he delivered his famous series of "non-lectures." In *i:six non-lectures* (1953), Cummings beautifully described 104 Irving:

> *My own home faced the Cambridge world as a finely and solidly constructed mansion, preceded by a large oval lawn and ringed with an imposing white-pine hedge. Just in front of the house itself stood two huge appletrees; and faithfully, every spring, these giants lifted their worlds of fragrance toward the room where I breathed and dreamed. . . .*

> *One of the many wonderful things about a home is that it can be as lively as you please without ever becoming public. The big Cambridge house was in this respect, as in all other respects, a true home.*

On the white picket fence across the street, at 95 Irving, another Cambridge Historical Commission plaque marks the house where **William James** (1842–1910), Henry's brother, lived between 1889 and 1910. Like Henry, the man heralded as the Father of Modern Psychology did not spend his early life in Cambridge. Born in New York City and raised in Europe and Newport, Rhode Island, William briefly pursued painting before entering Harvard Medical School and the world of science.

Julia Child on Irving Street and Fannie Farmer

I'm a Californian. In World War II, my husband, Paul, and I were in China, and Ceylon, and all kinds of places, and we decided rather than live in California, we would live in the Boston area where Paul grew up. I think that was 1956, and we bought the house on Irving Street for $35,000. It's the nicest neighborhood. It's easy to get to the Square. The house has a great big kitchen, and a great big room that Paul could use because he was a painter and wood-carver and photographer. Three of my TV series have been done in this kitchen.

It's an historic house that was built by Josiah Royce, a very famous philosopher in his time. Then E. E. Cummings was across the street—William James lived two or three houses down—and, of course, we have the Schlesinger House up at the corner here. Around the corner is the famous John Kenneth Galbraith, on Francis Street. José Luis Sert, the architect, who was about five feet tall, lived about a block from the Galbraiths. One of the great neighborhood sights was seeing him and Galbraith—what is he, six-ten?—talking to each other.

This is a very free community and there are so many interesting people. In Concord we have the inspiration for the Culinary Historians of Boston, Barbara Wheaton. She's a marvelous person. Then you have that Schlesinger Library at Harvard, which has one of the best culinary collections in the country. The academics don't know much about the culinary arts or gastronomy, and you have to push them to show them this is a serious discipline.

Was I influenced by Fannie Farmer? I think she had an influence on everybody, because she was the first one who actually did measurements. I used her recipe for fudge when I was just a kiddie. Her *Boston Cooking-School Cook Book* was our cookbook, when I was way out in California! I visited her gravesite here at Mount Auburn. I still use her when I want to do real American cooking.

From an interview by Susan Wilson with Julia Child

William James

In 1872, William James became a lecturer in physiology (1872–1873) and anatomy (1873–1876) at the medical school. While battling his own physical weakness and a nervous condition, James also battled the narrowness of Harvard's educational discipline, moving in and around the fields of medicine, physiology, philosophy, and psychology. In the lectures, articles, and books that he wrote over the next half century—such as *The Principles of Psychology* (1890), *Varieties of Religious Experience* (1902), *Pragmatism* (1907), and *A Pluralistic Universe* (1909)—James developed many of the concepts underlying modern psychology and philosophy, including pragmatism, radical empiricism, and stream of consciousness.

Continue on Irving Street to Kirkland, then turn right onto Kirkland and left onto Quincy. Passing Memorial Hall, continue on Quincy across Cambridge Street and Broadway. Take a right through the second gate into **Harvard Yard,** passing Emerson Hall on your left. This route was followed by Robert Lowell and commemorated in "T.S. Eliot" from "Writers" (*Notebook,* 1971):

> *Caught between two streams of traffic, in the gloom*
> *of Memorial Hall and Harvard's war-dead. . . . And he:*
> *'Don't you loathe to be compared with your relatives?*
> *I do. I've just found two of mine reviewed by Poe.*
> *He wiped the floor with them . . . and I was delighted.'*

Harvard Yard *(see image on page 98)* is impressive, both contemporary in its bustle and historic in its setting and structures. Equally impressive, however, is the number of graduates of international stature who have walked through here early in their educational journeys. The list of writers and thinkers who studied, taught, lectured, listened, argued, dropped out, or otherwise were affiliated with Harvard over the centuries is enough to fill several volumes.

Middlesex [County] is sacred territory,
because it contains the city of Cambridge, home of Harvard,
the center of the center and the hub of the hub.

—UPTON SINCLAIR, *BOSTON* (1928)

Graduates renowned for their writings would surely include Increase Mather (Class of 1656), Samuel Sewall (1671), Cotton Mather (1678), Thomas Prince (1707), Edward Everett (1811), William Hickling Prescott (1814), George Bancroft (1817), Ralph Waldo Emerson (1821), Oliver Wendell Holmes (1829), John Lothrop Motley (1831), Theodore Parker (1836), Henry David Thoreau (1837), Richard Henry Dana, Jr. (1837), James Russell Lowell (1838), Francis Parkman (1844), Henry Adams (1858), William James (M.D., 1869), Owen Wister (1882), George Santayana (1886), Bernard Berenson (1887), W. E. B. Du Bois (1890), Van Wyck Brooks (Class of 1908, graduated 1907), Samuel Eliot Morison (1908), T. S. Eliot (Class of 1910, graduated 1909; A.M. 1911), Conrad Aiken (Class of 1911, graduated 1912), Robert Benchley (Class of 1912, graduated 1913), E. E. Cummings (1915), J. P. Marquand (1915), John Dos Passos (1916), David McCord (1921), James Agee (1932), Daniel Boorstin (1934), Howard Nemerov (1941), Norman Mailer (1943), Justin Kaplan (Class of 1945, graduated 1944), Frank O'Hara (1950), Donald Hall (1951), Michael Halberstam (1953), John Updike (1954), Helen Vendler (Ph.D. 1960), and Michael Crichton (1964; M.D. 1969).

(Many more women obviously belong in this group. They appear later in the tour, when you visit the former Radcliffe College and the Schlesinger Library.)

Meanwhile, talented writers in every discipline have also taught at Harvard. Among them are ballad collector Francis James Child, philosopher William James, art historian Charles Eliot Norton, poet and linguist Henry Wadsworth Longfellow, scientist Louis Agassiz, playwright George Pierce Baker, and critic Helen Vendler. Screenwriter Spike Lee was a visiting lecturer for a semester.

Pulitzer Prize–winning historians like Oscar Handlin, Samuel Eliot Morison, Bernard Bailyn, and Arthur M. Schlesinger, Jr., have taught at Harvard, as have Pulitzer or Nobel Prize–winning poets like T. S. Eliot, Archibald MacLeish, Robert Lowell, Robert Frost, Elizabeth Bishop, and Seamus Heaney.

And the list goes on. . . .

Harry Elkins Widener Memorial Room,
Widener Library

The most imposing structure in Harvard Yard is the **Harry Elkins Widener Memorial Library,** the heart of the largest academic library in the world. Widener's gargantuan Corinthian columns and distinctive classical exterior were the choice of his mother, Eleanor Elkins Widener, who donated the library in memory of her son (Harvard Class of 1907), who went down with the *Titanic* in 1912. Today, Widener holds some 50 miles of bookshelves and 3.5 million volumes.

Harvard's extensive library system—with more than ninety subdivisions, stretching from Cambridge to Washington, D.C., and Villi I Tatti, Italy—had humble beginnings. The original library was already begun when **John Harvard** (1607–1638) died; Harvard often (erroneously) gets credit for starting the library, since he donated half his estate plus his personal collection of books—329 titles in 400 volumes—to the two-year-old college. Over the next century, the library's holdings grew tenfold—then virtually disappeared overnight. In the Great Fire of January 24, 1764, most of the school's 5,000-volume library was lost. The happy exceptions were 404 books, many of which were checked out or overdue at the time, including only one from John Harvard's original library, *The Christian Warfare Against the Devil, World, and Flesh*.

Widener's immediate predecessor was Gore Hall (1841). A popular landmark commemorated on the seal of the City of Cambridge, Gore Hall could barely keep up with the college's acquisitions. In 1877 an east wing was built, at a cost of $90,000, with six tiers of stacks that could hold 300,000 volumes. These were the first modern library stacks, where bookshelves formed part of a metal framework resting directly on the building's foundation, while supporting openwork floors and a roof.

Gore Hall was demolished in 1913 to make way for the vast Widener, which opened in 1915. Among its prestigious collections are a 1623 edition of Shakespeare's folios and a Gutenberg Bible.

Before leaving the subject of Bibles, note that Harvard College was responsible for producing the first version of the Bible ever printed in North America. In 1663, presses in Harvard's Indian College—a building in the Yard demolished in 1698—created the 1,200-page Indian Bible, translated into the Algonquin dialect by "the Apostle to the Indians," the **Reverend John Eliot** (1604–1690).

According to Samuel Eliot Morison, the "Indian Bible" had trouble with words or concepts that had no Algonquin equivalent. The word for "*virgin*," for example, was either little used or little known. Hence, whenever it appeared in the text, Eliot replaced it with the closest word he could find, the Algonquin term for "a chaste young man."

Facing the entrance to Widener, turn right and walk around to the front of University Hall.

Here is one of the Yard's most prized possessions: a bronze statue of the seated **John Harvard**, sculpted by Daniel Chester French in 1884. French is best remembered for his *Minute Man* at North Bridge in Concord, Massachusetts, his seated Lincoln, the centerpiece of the Lincoln Memorial in Washington, D.C., and *Death and the Sculptor*, at the entrance to Forest Hills Cemetery.

The popular John Harvard statue, inscribed "John Harvard, Founder, 1638," has been dubbed "the Statue of Three Lies": (1) the image is not of Harvard, since no known rendering of him existed; French used Sherman Hoar of Concord, a student chosen at random, as a model; (2) Harvard College was founded in 1636, not

John Harvard, Harvard Yard

Strange interlude!
Yes, our lives are merely strange dark interludes
in the electrical display of God the Father.

—EUGENE O'NEILL, *STRANGE INTERLUDE* (1928)

1638; and (3) John was not a founder of the college but its first benefactor, who, as noted before, donated his library and half of his estate to the school.

Directly across the way is **Massachusetts Hall**, where **George Pierce Baker** taught his **47 Workshop** in playwriting that was attended by such nascent talents as Thomas Wolfe and Eugene O'Neill. Massachusetts Hall—which houses the university's president, provost, and vice-president—has not been used for classrooms since the turn of the last century. Most of the structure, incidentally, continues to serve as a dormitory—its orginal purpose when built in 1720.

Return to Harvard Square and the main driving route of the Literary Trail by taking any of the nearby paths through the brick gateways back to Mass. Ave.

Pick up the main route of the Literary Trail at the center of Harvard Square. Brattle Street begins across from the Out of Town newsstand, then takes an abrupt right in front of One Brattle Square. Just after the Brattle Theatre on the left is 42 Brattle, a yellow clapboard building that is now the Cambridge Center for Adult Education.

This is the **1727 Brattle House**, originally one of a series of Loyalist farms that stretched from here to Fresh Pond Parkway. The number of Loyalists who lived in spectacular Brattle Street homes during the revolutionary era gave Brattle Street the name of Tory Row. **Margaret Fuller**, a Cambridge native, feminist, transcendentalist, and editor of the *Dial*, lived here in 1832.

Ahead on the left (and also part of the Cambridge Center for Adult Education), 54 Brattle Street was the home of Dexter Pratt, who was immortalized by his neighbor, poet Henry Wadsworth Longfellow, in "The Village Blacksmith" (1839):

Under a spreading chestnut tree
The village smithy stands
The smith a mighty man he is
With large and sinewy hands,
And the muscles of his brawny arms
Are strong as iron bands.

Today, the **Blacksmith House** continues its literary connection as the home of the **Blacksmith House Poetry Series**. Founded in 1973 by Gail Mazur and sponsored by the Cambridge Center for Adult Education, this nationally known poetry series offers a variety of contemporary poetry and fiction programs. Readings by authors and poets, open to the public for a modest fee, are held on Monday evenings from October through May.

Farther down on the left is 60 Brattle Street, **Harvard's Loeb Drama Center** and the **American Repertory Theatre**. Director, drama critic, and playwright **Robert Brustein** (b. 1927), who was both founder and longtime artistic director of the ART, was elected to the American Academy of Arts and Sciences in 1999. An English professor at Harvard, he has served as drama critic for the *New Republic* since 1959. He has written numerous plays, as well as books of commentary and criticism on the theater. Following Brustein's retirement from the ART (2002), the Howard Gotlieb Archival Research Center at Harvard University (once called Special Collections) acquired his personal archive, which includes manuscripts, correspondence, photos, and other memorabilia.

Continuing down Brattle Street, you will pass through part of the Radcliffe College campus, now known as the **Radcliffe Institute for Advanced Study**, of Harvard University. In 1879 Harvard's professors—who taught only men—were asked to make accommodations for instructing women as well. By 1894, the Society for the Collegiate Instruction for Women had been named Radcliffe College, after the donor of Harvard's first seventeenth-century endowment, Ann Radcliffe.

Among the significant buildings here are Agassiz House, named for **Elizabeth Cary Agassiz,** Radcliffe's first president, and Longfellow Hall, which honors **Alice Longfellow**. The eldest daughter of the poet, Alice was heavily involved in the development of education for women at Radcliffe.

Over the past century, countless writers have been affiliated with Radcliffe, including the inimitable **Gertrude Stein** (Class of 1898), historical writer **Barbara Tuchman** (1933), journalist and author **Phyllis Schlafly** (1945), novelist **Rona Jaffe** (1951), Canadian author **Margaret Atwood** (1962), playwright **Honor Moore** (1967), and feminist **Susan Faludi** (1981). Among Radcliffe's many poets are **Maxine Kumin** (1946, M.A. 1948), **Adrienne Rich** (1951), **Phyllis Koestenbaum** (1952), and **Anne Sexton** (Radcliffe Institute, 1961–1963).

On the corner of Brattle and James streets, behind the brick gate at 3 James, is the Arthur and Elizabeth **Schlesinger Library on the History of Women in America**. A variety of women scholars, writers, reformers, critics, and social activists have placed their papers here,

Radcliffe Yard

including classicist **Edith Hamilton**, novelist of the Harlem Renaissance **Dorothy West** (*The Living Is Easy*), playwright **Eve Merriam**, feminists **Charlotte Perkins Gilman** (*The Yellow Wallpaper*), **Betty Friedan**, and **Pauli Murray**, abolitionist **Harriet Beecher Stowe**, novelist and social reformer **Margaret Deland**, and poet **June Jordan**. The library also collects the papers of food writers, notably **Julia Child**, **Irma Rombauer** (*The Joy of Cooking*), **M. F. K. Fisher**, and **Elizabeth David**.

Directly across Brattle Street is the right-hand driveway of **Greenleaf House**, at 76 Brattle. Built in 1859 and once the home of Mary Longfellow and her husband, James Greenleaf, it became the official residence of Radcliffe presidents after 1913.

Follow the brick wall on the right down a small footpath to the rear to find a quiet treasure: a modest Roman fountain with a stream of water pouring from a lion's mouth into a tiled pool. On the ivy-covered wall behind is a pair of plaques—one in Braille, one in English—placed by **Helen Keller** (1880–1968), a Radcliffe alumna:

> *In memory of ANNE SULLIVAN, teacher extraordinary—who, begin-ning with the word water, opened to the girl Helen Keller the world of sight and sound through touch. Beloved companion through Radcliffe College, 1900–1904.*

Helen Keller was unable to see, hear, or speak since infancy. In *The Story of My Life* (1924), she explains how Sullivan taught her the word *water:*

> *We walked down the path to the well-house, attracted by the fra-grance of the honeysuckle with which it was covered. Some one was drawing water and my teacher placed my hand under the spout. As the cool stream gushed over one hand she spelled into the other the word water, first slowly, then rapidly. I*

Helen Keller, Annie Sullivan, and Edward Everett Hale, 1903

---

stood still, my whole attention fixed upon the motions of her fingers. Suddenly I felt a misty consciousness as of something forgotten—a thrill of returning thought; and somehow the mystery of language was revealed to me. I knew then that "w-a-t-e-r" meant the wonderful cool something that was flowing over my hand. That living word awakened my soul, gave it light, hope, joy, set it free!

At the intersection of Brattle and Mason, Ash Street veers off to the left. If you are on foot, walk down this shady and quietly elegant street, lined with sturdy white fences, old-growth arbors, brick sidewalks, and well-tended gardens.

Just past Ash Street Place, on the left, a Cambridge Historical Commission plaque on 14 Ash notes that the poet **T. S. (Thomas Stearns) Eliot** (1888–1965) lived here in 1913 and 1914, while teaching philosophy at Harvard.

Eliot was already familiar with Harvard when he returned to lecture. A member of the Class of 1910, he graduated a year early, then went on to complete his master's degree by 1911. Though he could trace his ancestry back to colonial New England, Eliot was born to a poet and a businessman in St. Louis, Missouri. His poetic sensibility, however, required a different terrain than Cambridge had to offer, and he fled to England in 1914. There, Eliot found a bad marriage, Ezra Pound, a nervous breakdown, and the muses he had been seeking. Soon he wrote *Ezra Pound: His Metric and Poetry* (1917), *Prufrock and Other Observations* (1917), *Poems* (1920), *The Waste Land* (1922), and his first volume of criticism, *The Sacred Wood* (1920). When not writing reviews and poems—or finding fascination in the interplay of church and state—he periodically taught school, clerked in a bank, and edited literary journals. Though he became a British citizen, he returned to Harvard in 1932—his first trip across the Atlantic since his departure. His lectures there became *The Use of Poetry and the Use of Criticism* (1933).

Eliot went on to become the twentieth century's most celebrated English-language poet and was awarded both the Nobel Prize for Literature and the British Order of Merit in 1948. Curiously, one of the poet's weakest works won him undying fame when, in 1981, the musical version of *Old Possum's Book of Practical Cats* (1939) opened on the London stage. The extravaganza called *Cats* has been a popular mainstay of American stages ever since.

If the Old Corner Bookstore was the gathering place for mid-nineteenth-century writers in Boston, the elegant home of **Henry Wadsworth Longfellow** (1807-1882) at 105 Brattle Street—today Longfellow National Historic Site—was an equally powerful magnet in Cambridge. Built in 1759 for the wealthy Tory John Vassall, Jr., this private house served as General George Washington's headquarters for nine months in 1775 when he took charge of the Continental Army. In the 1830s, when the young Longfellow was hired to teach

Longfellow House with Henry Wadsworth Longfellow and his daughter Edith, 1878

modern languages at Harvard, the house belonged to Elizabeth Craigie, the widow of Andrew Craigie. Longfellow first rented two rooms here in 1837. Six years later, Longfellow and his new wife, Fanny Appleton, were given the home as a wedding gift from Fanny's father.

One of the nineteenth century's most popular poets, scholars, and educators, Longfellow was a native of Portland, Maine. Two years after publishing his first poem, the fifteen-year-old joined Nathaniel Hawthorne and Franklin Pierce at Bowdoin College, in Brunswick,

Maine. His college work completed, Longfellow studied romance languages abroad, then returned to Bowdoin as its librarian and professor of modern languages before moving to Cambridge.

Once lodged in the Craigie mansion and at Harvard, Longfellow, along with his family and friends, proved integral to the development of American culture and traditions. The voluminous poetic works he completed during his forty-five years on Brattle Street include "The Courtship of Miles Standish," "The Village Blacksmith," "The Song of Hiawatha," "The Wreck of the Hesperus," and "Paul Revere's Ride."

The constant flow of Longfellow's international friends and guests included the finest thinkers and writers of his day—from his collegemate Nathaniel Hawthorne and transcendentalist Ralph Waldo Emerson to abolitionist Charles Sumner and many of Boston's most powerful citizens. Longfellow's wife, Fanny, was herself considered a noteworthy, though unpublished, art and literary critic.

To this assemblage Longfellow brought intellect, art, camaraderie, and joy. William Dean Howells, in *Literary Friends and Acquaintance* (1900), recalled his unique presence:

When he walked, he had kind of a spring in his gait, as if now and again a buoyant thought lifted him from the ground. It was fine to meet him coming down a Cambridge street; you felt that the encounter made you a part of literary history, and set you apart with him for the moment from the poor and mean.

Longfellow's first wife, Mary Storer Potter, had a miscarriage and died after four years of marriage. Fanny Appleton died prematurely as well, from burns incurred in a tragic fire at their home. The familiar vision we have of Longfellow today—the gentle sage with the flowing white beard—was partly a result of that fire. Suffering burns on his face as he attempted to smother the flames on his beloved Fanny, he later hid his scars with facial hair.

Writing to Annie and James T. Fields in 1861, Hawthorne expressed his disbelief at the event:

> *How does Longfellow bear this terrible misfortune? How are his own injuries? . . . I cannot at all reconcile this calamity to my sense of fitness. One would think that there ought to have been no deep sorrow in a man like him; and now comes this blackest of shadows, which no sunshine hereafter can ever penetrate! I shall be afraid ever to meet him again; he cannot again be the man that I have known. . . .*

The likable Longfellow was always careful to stand aside from the political storms of the era. He admired revolutionary heroes of the safe and distant past and deliberately chose to put his study in the bedroom once used by General George Washington. His close friendship with Charles Sumner, however, may have inspired him to write *Poems on Slavery* (1842). Few of his contemporaries criticized Longfellow or his work, save the enigmatic Edgar Allan Poe, who wrote off most Hub residents as provincial "Frogpondians."

Today the mid-Georgian mansion is inspirational and the setting stunning: it provides grand views from Brattle Street and faces Longfellow Park, which slopes down to the river. When the house is open seasonally for tours, visitors can see its nineteenth-century furnishings, artwork, some ten thousand books, and the dining room table around which important literary figures once gathered. You can also imbibe the aura of a home linked to three centuries of history and a site that has inspired countless generations of writers.

In Longfellow's day, the park across the street offered him a clear view of the Charles. That view is long gone, alas, though the park is still a beautiful place to stroll and a favorite spot for picnickers and dog walkers. The long stretch of green off Brattle Street leads to a short staircase and a memorial below. There, a bust of Longfellow (1914) by Daniel Chester French is surrounded by a bas-relief by Henry Bacon that depicts six of Longfellow's heroes: Miles Standish, Sandalphon, the Village Blacksmith, the Spanish Student, Evangeline, and Hiawatha.

Longfellow's literary reach, incidentally, continues well into the twenty-first century. Among the poet's many credits was introducing the literary genius of Dante to the English-speaking world, by composing the first American translation of *Inferno* in 1867. In 2003 Dante scholar and Harvard graduate Matthew Pearl brought Longfellow and his nineteenth-century literary colleagues alive once more in a mystery novel called *The Dante Club*. The *Baltimore Sun* raved, "*The Dante Club* is delightful and suspenseful, an unexpected story about Boston's literary giants tracking a post-Civil War serial killer. . . . [It's] a unique, ambitious, entertaining read, a historical thriller with a poetic streak."

An excellent walking tour of literary Cambridge can be found in *Footprints on the Sands of Time: Longfellow's 19th Century Cambridge*. Published in 1996 by the Eastern National Park and Monument Association, it offers stellar insights, images, stories, and literary quotations from America's Golden Age of Literature.

Beyond the Longfellow House is 121 Brattle, the former home of **Joseph Worcester** (1784–1865). Like Longfellow, Worcester was once a lodger at the widow Craigie's. He was the *other* dictionary-maker, renowned in the nineteenth century for his huge, unabridged *English Dictionary* (1843), which sought to standardize the English language and make it accessible to all. Today Worcester's name is overshadowed by that of his contemporary Noah Webster, who developed *Webster's Dictionary*.

Continuing down Brattle Street, filled with majestic homes and grand yards, you will pass Sparks, Riedesel, and Appleton Streets. Just past Appleton on the right, at 159 Brattle, is the **Hooper-Lee-Nichols House** (1680s; remodeled ca. 1760), the home of the **Cambridge Historical Society**. At 165 Brattle once lived the master of quotations, **John Bartlett** (1820–1905), when not at work in his University Book Store in Harvard Square.

Farther down Brattle Street, at 192, was the family home of **Josephine Preston Peabody** (1874–1922), and her husband, Harvard professor **Lionel Marks**. Renowned as a poetic dramatist—whose plays included *Fortune and Men's Eyes* (1900), *Marlowe* (1901), *The Piper* (1909), and *Portrait of Mrs. W.* (1922)—Peabody saw her first poem printed in the *Atlantic* when she was nineteen. After attending Girls' Latin School in Boston and Radcliffe College in Cambridge, where she was a special student for two years, Peabody's first book, *Old Greek Folk Stories*, was published by Houghton Mifflin. From 1901 to 1903, she taught poetry and literature at Wellesley College. In her later years, Peabody was a crusader for liberal causes such as women's suffrage, laborers' rights, pacifism, and relief for war refugees. She died at forty-eight, after a two-week coma brought on by hardening of the arteries of the brain.

Take a left off Brattle Street onto Elmwood and walk down to the large, elegant estate on the right, at 33 Elmwood. Now known as the **Oliver-Gerry-Lowell House**, this 1767 Tory mansion was once the home of Vice President Elbridge Gerry. Today it is the official residence of the president of Harvard.

Its most famous resident, however, was the poet, essayist, and diplomat **James Russell Lowell** (1819-1891), who spent his entire life at Elmwood. Lowell belonged to the New England Lowells, who, along with the Lawrences, ran much of nineteenth-century New England, having come to prominence and fortune through textile mills. The Lowell family produced its fair share of lawyers and judges, clerics, business and political leaders, and scholars.

James Russell Lowell had a number of careers open to him. After graduating from Harvard and choosing Maria White as his wife, he rejected medicine, the ministry, and the law to pursue literary and political writing, with a penchant for poetic forms and abolitionist arguments. Among his best works were four that were published in 1848: *Poems*, *The Vision of Sir Launfal*, *A Fable for Critics*, and *The Bigelow Papers*—the latter a witty

James Russell Lowell

satire on the wildly unpopular Mexican War. Lowell went on to influence and nurture other writers when he succeeded Longfellow as professor of Modern Languages at Harvard, became the first editor of the *Atlantic Monthly*, and served as an editor of the *North American Review*. He was also a diplomat, both in Spain and the Court of St. James in London.

Throughout his life, the distinctive house at 33 Elmwood, with its impressive double chimneys, was a gentle muse to Lowell:

My Elmwood chimneys seem crooning to me,
As of old in their moody, minor key,
And out of the past the hoarse wind blows.

Muses, of course, come and go. Like any other writer, Lowell endured large stretches of time when ideas rarely appeared, as noted in this letter, reprinted in *Memories of a Hostess* (1922):

From my study, this first day for three weeks without a drowsy pain in my knowledge box, I really feel a little lively, and wonder at myself. But don't be alarmed—it won't last, any more than money does, or principle in a politician, or hair, or popular favor—or paper.

Since Elmwood Road is no longer a through street to Mount Auburn, turn around and return to Brattle Street. To stay on the main route of the Literary Trail, bear right onto Brattle. To take a walking tour "Off the Beaten Path," take a left onto Brattle and follow it the few blocks to its end. Cross Mount Auburn Street to reach the neo-Egyptian entrance of Mount Auburn Cemetery.

Mount Auburn Cemetery: A Walking Tour
Approximate Time: 1–3 Hours

Cemeteries—like homes, bookshops, lecture halls, and hotels—were gathering places for the literary world of Boston. Certainly, friends and colleagues came together at the funerals of beloved kith and kin. But they also often chose the same cemeteries, and sometimes the same sections of those cemeteries, for their eternal rest. As a result, there may be no larger gathering of late American literary figures than Mount Auburn Cemetery in Cambridge. Founded in 1831 as the first rural garden cemetery in America, and today a National Historic Landmark, Mount Auburn even had a literary beginning.

For many decades, the woods between the road to Watertown and the Charles River had been a popular site for Harvard students to wander and muse. Ralph Waldo Emerson and, years later, Robert Frost walked here often, with a book or friend in hand. Though properly known as Stone's Farm, the land was called "Sweet Auburn" by the students, after Oliver Goldsmith's poem "The Deserted Village" (1770):

> *Sweet Auburn! loveliest village of the plain,*
> *Where health and plenty cheer'd the labouring swain,*
> *Where smiling spring its earliest visit paid,*
> *And parting summer's lingering blooms delay'd:*
> *Dear lovely bowers of innocence and ease,*
> *Seats of my youth, when every sport could please,*
> *How often have I loiter'd o'er thy green,*
> *Where humble happiness endear'd each scene!*

When the land was purchased by a group of Bostonians and developed as a cemetery, the name Auburn remained. So too did the community's interest in wandering amid these wooded slopes while honoring their friends and heroes with tokens of remembrance.

From its earliest years, Mount Auburn Cemetery was the preferred resting place of hundreds of famous women and men. Maps of the cemetery, available for a nominal fee at the front gate and main office, note the location of many of these significant residents and their memorials. Audio tours, both for driving and walking, can be rented or purchased at the entrance gate as well.

Among the members of the literary world memorialized here are many people we've met elsewhere on the Literary Trail, such as **Henry Wadsworth Longfellow, Julia Ward Howe, James T.** and **Annie Fields, Fannie Farmer, Amy Lowell, James Russell Lowell, Francis Parkman, Oliver Wendell Holmes, John Bartlett, Hannah Adams, Josephine St. Pierre Ruffin, Isabella Stewart Gardner,** and **David McCord. Charles Little** and **James Brown** are here too—the namesakes of Little, Brown publishers—with matching brownstone Gothic monuments on adjoining lots.

Most of these residents lie below their finely sculpted monuments. Other markers, known as cenotaphs, are memorials to the dead that do not contain their earthly remains. **Margaret Fuller (Ossoli)**, for example, was lost in a shipwreck with her husband and child. Though her baby was found and interred here, his parents' bodies were never recovered. The memorial to **Robert Gould Shaw** is a cenotaph as well, since his body remains in the mass grave at Fort Wagner, South Carolina, where he and his soldiers fell.

Other people of letters at Mount Auburn include **William Alfred** (Harvard professor and playwright), **Bernard Malamud** (*Rembrandt's Hat*), **R. Buckminster Fuller** (*Synergetics*), **Eleanor Hodgman Porter** (*Pollyanna*), **Thomas Bulfinch** (*Bulfinch's Mythology*), and **Mary Baker Eddy**, founder of the Christian Science Church, who wrote the essential book on spirituality and healing, *Science and Health with Key to the Scriptures* (1875).

Perhaps less familiar is **Harriet Jacobs**, whose autobiography, *Incidents in the Life of a Slave Girl: Written by Herself* (1861), was a groundbreaking and controversial work. Born into slavery in North Carolina, Jacobs escaped to the North and was hidden for years until her freedom was finally purchased in 1852.

Mount Auburn became such a prestigious address for its permanent residents that it was continually praised—and mocked—in both prose and poetry. Here, some long-forgotten bard muses about pompous landscapes in "A True Bostonian," a popular poem from the turn of the twentieth century:

A soul from Earth to Heaven went
To whom the Saint as he drew near
Said, "Sir, what claims do you present,
To us to be admitted here?"

"In Boston I was born and bred,
And in her schools was educated;
I afterwards at Harvard read,
And was with honors graduated.
In Trinity a pew I owned
Where Brooks is held in such respect;
And the society is known
To be the cream of the select.
In fair Nahant a charming spot,
I own a villa, lawn, arcades,
And last a handsome burial lot
In dead Mount Auburn's hallowed shades."
St. Peter mused, and shook his head,
Then as a gentle sigh he drew,
"Go back to Boston, friend," he said,
"Heaven isn't good enough for you."

It should be noted that degrees from Boston Latin and Harvard, a pew at Trinity Church, and a summer home at Nahant were not in the pedigree of most of Mount Auburn's occupants. Henry Wadsworth Longfellow is indeed buried here; so too is "The Village Blacksmith" about whom he wrote.

A brief foray into **Cambridge Cemetery** next door shows that not every literary Cantabrigian opted to spend the hereafter at Mount Auburn.

Leaving through the front gate of Mount Auburn, take a right onto Mount Auburn Street, then another right onto Coolidge Avenue. The main gate of Cambridge Cemetery is a half mile down on the left, marked by stone pillars. Maps of the cemetery are available at the office by the front gate, though they do not note specific graves.

Head up Summit Avenue and bear left onto the outer road of the cemetery, passing the playing fields of Shady Hill and Buckingham, Browne & Nichols Schools. Curve back onto Prospect Avenue to find two similar lots, both backed by low brick walls. One marks **William Dean Howells** and his family, the other the **Jameses**, including William, Henry, and Alice.

Thomas Wentworth Higginson—the abolitionist, author, and correspondent of Emily Dickinson—is buried at the junction of Riverview, Lawn, and Prospect. Sadly, the site seems forgotten, for it is crowded by such useful items as a faucet and a trash can.

Robert Frost

If you have traveled as far as Mount Auburn and Cambridge cemeteries, return to Brattle Street and walk back toward Harvard Square. Take a left at Appleton Street, then a right onto Brewster.

A Cambridge Historical Commission plaque notes that 35 Brewster, a wide double house, was the home of **Robert Frost** (1874–1963) for the last two decades of his life.

Though born in San Francisco, Robert Frost became known as the quintessential New England poet. After years of different activities—from bobbin- and shoe-making to teaching and farming—Frost moved to England and published his first book of poems, *A Boy's Will* (1913). After his successful publication of *North of Boston* in 1914, Frost was on his way back to America—and on his way to being recognized as a significant American poet.

Frost's writing was not particularly innovative. When asked what he thought of free verse in an interview with *Newsweek* in 1957, he replied, "I'd just as soon play tennis with the net down." Still, Frost broke through the transcendentalist and Victorian values of the nineteenth century to write with a modern sensibility in plain, readable rhyme. His best lines were multilayered, deeply American, and emotionally restrained. They touched the hearts and minds of generations of Americans—and made Frost the logical choice to read his poem "The Gift Outright" at John F. Kennedy's inauguration in 1961.

Like Longfellow a century before him, Frost became the nation's most recognized and honored man of poetry. He was awarded countless prizes, including Pulitzers for *New Hampshire* (1924), *Collected Poems* (1931), *A Further Range* (1937), and *A Witness Tree* (1943). Only his circle of friends knew of his fierce competitiveness and—in his later years—eccentric irritability. One night in 1938, for example, Frost set fire to a stack of papers to disrupt a poetry reading by his colleague Archibald MacLeish.

Frost taught at Amherst College between 1916 and 1938. After the death of his wife, he moved to 88 Mount Vernon Street, overlooking

I shall be telling this with a sigh
Somewhere ages and ages hence:
Two roads diverged in a wood, and I—
I took the one less traveled by,
And that has made all the
difference.

—ROBERT FROST, "THE ROAD NOT TAKEN" (1916)

Louisburg Square. Then, after his son's suicide, Frost's friends and fans formed the Ralph Waldo Emerson poetry fellowship at Harvard and enticed the poet to lecture in Harvard's English Department. Frost bought the left half of this house on Brewster Street in 1941 and lived here when not residing in Vermont or Florida.

Walk to the end of Brewster and take a right onto Sparks, then a hard left onto Craigie Street at the major intersection. Take a quick left down Buckingham, past the elementary school campus of the private Buckingham, Browne & Nichols School.

Perched on a hill on the left, 29 Buckingham was the home of **Thomas Wentworth Higginson** (1823–1911), whose many roles included author, essayist, abolitionist, minister, Civil War officer, and correspondent of Emily Dickinson. Born in Cambridge, the precocious, happy, and well-read Higginson entered Harvard at thirteen, was elected to Phi Beta Kappa at sixteen, graduated at seventeen, then went on to Harvard Divinity School. Though he entered the ministry—tending flocks in Newburyport and, later, Worcester, Massachusetts—he proved a radical nonconformist and inveterate man of action.

While many of Higginson's literary peers of the 1850s opposed slavery, most were content to document their concerns in books, journals, lectures, and petitions. Hence, in 1854, when an escaped slave named

Thomas Wentworth Higginson, 1903

If I feel physically as if the top of my head
were taken off, I know that is poetry.

—EMILY DICKINSON, CITED IN THOMAS WENTWORTH HIGGINSON,
"EMILY DICKINSON'S LETTERS," *ATLANTIC MONTHLY,* OCTOBER 1891

Anthony Burns was arrested in Boston—and threatened with extradition to his southern master under the Fugitive Slave Law—Richard Henry Dana offered to defend Burns in court, while pacifist poet John Greenleaf Whittier called for nonviolent resistance.

Higginson's response was singular. Not satisfied with the slow course of justice, he led a small group of radicals and stormed the U.S. Courthouse in Boston, armed with a huge battering ram, axes, revolvers, and butcher's cleavers. Though their mission failed—and Burns was returned to slavery, at least for a time—Higginson received a saber slash on his chin that he displayed proudly for the rest of his life.

Higginson continued his life of left-wing politics and adamant action by backing the efforts of John Brown and leading a regiment of black soldiers in the Civil War. Returning home, he filled his days with writing, teaching, and a perennial commitment to social reform—especially equal rights for blacks and women. Among his works are *Army Life in a Black Regiment* (1870), biographies of Margaret Fuller (1884), Whittier (1902), and Longfellow (1902), and a fascinating autobiography, *Cheerful Yesterdays* (1898).

Higginson is best known, however, for his literary relationship with **Emily Dickinson** (1830–1886). In 1862, the self-proclaimed "Belle of Amherst" wrote to Higginson after reading one of his articles in the *Atlantic.* She began her letter, "Mr. Higginson—are you too deeply occupied to say if my verse is alive?" Higginson puzzled over her "remarkable, though odd" form and content, then advised the young poet not to publish. Their correspondence continued over the next two decades, filled with encouragement and fondness. The reclusive, brilliant Dickinson sent Higginson a poem with every letter. It was not until after her death that her sister Lavinia and Mabel Loomis Todd, the wife of an Amherst professor, contacted Higginson anew and convinced him to help them publish the poems. Even then, Higginson felt compelled to alter some of the poet's

> *For me a work of fiction exists only insofar as it affords me what I shall bluntly call aesthetic bliss.*
>
> —VLADIMIR NABOKOV, "ON A BOOK ENTITLED LOLITA,"
> AFTERWORD TO *LOLITA* (1956)

rhyme, rhythm, lines, language, and punctuation—an error not corrected for many decades.

Though Dickinson is not usually associated with Boston or Cambridge, she did travel here twice during the Civil War era. In 1864 she stayed in Cambridgeport while seeing an eye specialist, Dr. Henry Williams, and in 1865 she returned for six months of treatments. Once home, however, she never left Amherst again. The poet had a need to stay close to home, as well as a disdain for so-called culture in Boston. In an 1851 letter to her brother Austin, she announced, "We don't care a fig for the museums, the stillness, or Jennie Lind."

Take Healy Street, on the right near Higginson's old home, to Parker Street, then turn right toward Buckingham in order to return to Craigie Street. As you proceed along Craigie, you'll pass the private Craigie Circle on your left.

Vladimir Nabokov (1899–1977) lived at 8 Craigie Circle between 1942 and 1948. Nabokov came from a wealthy Russian family, who fled their homeland toward the end of the Russian Revolution. Educated at Trinity College in Cambridge, England, Nabokov moved to America in 1940, became a U.S. citizen in 1945, and taught at Wellesley, then Cornell. His extraordinary lectures on Russian and European literature ended only when his success at writing allowed him to retire from the lectern.

Among Nabokov's many stylized and witty novels are *Laughter in the Dark* (1938), *Invitation to a Beheading* (1938), *The Real Life of Sebastian Knight* (1941), and *Lolita* (1958). His stories, poems, and lectures have also appeared in collected form. While living in Cambridge in the 1940s, Nabokov worked part-time at Harvard's Museum of Comparative Zoology. Since then, critics have dissected his works, seeking and analyzing his references to butterflies. *Nabokov's Butterflies* (2000), edited by Brian Boyd and Robert Michael Pyle, contains uncollected and unpublished writings that reflect Nabokov's two great passions, literature and lepidoptera.

Anne Bernays on
Literary Mist in Cambridge

It's difficult to live in Cambridge without acknowledging writers long gone whose essence adheres like the perfume they used to spray at you in expensive department stores.

Whether or not your own prose is anything like theirs, you feel an obligation to succeed at some level for their sake. Around the corner from where I live is the house of e. e. cummings, whose poetry, when I read it first in college, struck me as astonishing with its cubist syntax and deliberately skewed vision. It still seems fresh and minty.

Henry James, by any standard a towering figure for novelists, lived in Cambridge as a young man. Although he left thereafter, you can feel New England in his bones, even when he's writing about New Yorkers or Europeans. James burrowed into nuances of human temperament and reaction in a way you can only envy and try, palely, to emulate.

It's nice to think of Vladimir Nabokov sitting in a musty room at Harvard's Peabody Museum down the street, cataloguing his beloved butterflies. For me, Nabokov is the supreme prose artist of the twentieth century. To read one page of, say, *Speak, Memory*, is to be fueled for a week. *Lolita*, satire and love story, is matchless; *Pnin* a model of sweet humor.

Continue along Craigie Street and take a left onto Concord Avenue at the intersection. Just ahead on the left is 34 Concord, which now houses the fellowship program of Harvard University's **Radcliffe Institute for Advanced Study**. Each year some forty fellows from across the country and around the world come to the Radcliffe Institute to undertake groundbreaking work in a wide variety of academic disciplines and the creative arts. Through the fellowship program and public programming, the Institute sustains a continuing commitment to the study of women, gender, and society. Among the twelve hundred alumnae of the current Institute's predecessor—the Mary Ingraham Bunting Institute, which operated under the old Radcliffe College—are playwright Paula Vogel, journalist Christina Robb, historians Nell Painter and Jill Lepore, and writers Alice Walker, Jayne Anne Phillips, Sue Miller, Tillie Olsen, and Fae Myenne Ng. Poets Maxine Kumin, Patricia Cleary Miller, Jorie Graham, and Anne Sexton were also once Bunting fellows. Recent Radcliffe Institute fellows include authors Junot Diaz, Gish Jen, and Zadie Smith, lawyer-author Elizabeth Warren, sociologist-author Constance Ahrons, and numerous astrophysicists, historians, computer scientists, philosophers, and mathematicians.

Across the street, at 37 Concord Avenue, is the home of **William Dean Howells** (1837–1920), America's preeminent man of letters at the turn of the last century. Well known as the gentleman who replaced James T. Fields as editor of the *Atlantic Monthly*, Howells was also a novelist, poet, essayist, short story writer, and critic of considerable talent. His finest novel, *The Rise of Silas Lapham* (1885), is the classic account of the nouveau riche post–Civil War industrialist who couldn't buy his way into the culture of Boston Brahmins. *Silas Lapham*, as it turns out, portrayed a microcosm of Howell's ambivalent feelings about Boston and Bostonians.

Born in Ohio, Howells came to Boston in search of a literary mecca. In 1860, the twenty-three-year-old writer took a stagecoach to Concord, Massachusetts, and proceeded to introduce himself to Hawthorne, Thoreau, and Emerson. As fate would have it, the man who first sought literary culture in Boston eventually helped mold it. By 1866 he was an assistant editor at the *Atlantic* and by 1871, chief editor.

Howells became a magnet for other writers, both local and national. He befriended the James family as well as Oliver Wendell

Holmes, James Russell Lowell, Charles Eliot Norton, and Longfellow. He introduced the western writers Mark Twain and Bret Harte to the Saturday Club and came to live in all the right places—including Beacon Street and Louisburg Square in Boston, and Sacramento Street and Concord Avenue in Cambridge.

Howells was such an important literary figure in Boston that many historians equate his departure for New York in 1881 with the end of Boston as the literary hub of America. Surely Howells sensed that the center for books, magazines, and literature was starting to shift to Manhattan. Moreover, the intellectual institutions that drew him here in the first place—Harvard College, the Boston Athenaeum, and the *Atlantic Monthly*—could not offset his concerns about the new people he saw coming to Boston and Cambridge.

"All Ireland seems to be poured upon [us]," Howells wrote to Henry James in 1869, "and there is such a clamor of Irish children about us all day, that I suspect my 'exquisite English,' as I've seen it called in the papers, will yet be written with a brogue." This xenophobia and condescension that Howells and James shared toward Boston's new immigrant populations was, sadly, not unique among their peers.

The Literary Trail now moves from Cambridge to Concord, a lengthy route best taken by car or tour bus.

To get to the town of Concord, follow Concord Avenue to Route 2, past Fresh Pond Reservation. The paths and areas around the pond here are a favorite spot for joggers, walkers (with and without dogs), and bicyclists today. Almost a century ago, William Dean Howells and Henry James used to walk together here as well, discussing their work while watching the skaters—or boaters—on the pond, depending on the season.

Pass the Alewife "T" station, then bear left and continue on Route 2, now a highway. At the second set of lights after crossing I-95/128, where Route 2 takes a sharp left, continue straight ahead toward the center of Concord on the Cambridge Turnpike. The drive from Cambridge to Concord is generally around twenty minutes.

As you travel down this old **Cambridge Turnpike**, you are taking the route that Ralph Waldo Emerson and his friends rode—by carriage or stagecoach—on their regular outings to Lexington, Cambridge, and Boston. In the first decades of the nineteenth cen-

*I walk along the Mill Brook below Emerson's,
looking into it for some life. . . .
Perhaps what most moves us in winter is some
reminiscence of far-off summer. How we leap
by the side of the open brooks! What beauty in
the running brooks! What life! What society!
The cold is merely superficial; it is summer
still at the core, far, far within.*

—HENRY DAVID THOREAU, *JOURNAL* (1855)

---

tury, the stage from Concord to Boston took three hours in good
weather, up to five hours in bad. When the railroad was built in 1844,
it shortened the trip to an hour and became the writers' preferred
mode of transportation.

Crossing the Mill Brook, you will see the Concord Museum on the
right. Stop near the gazebo outside the museum, just before the intersection with Lexington Road. Directly across the street is the house
where Emerson lived from 1835 until his death in 1882.

N

Concord River

LOWELL RD.

MONUMENT ST.

MAIN ST.

BELKNAP ST.

MILL
DAM LN.

MARTIN RD.

7

10

WINDMILL
HILL RD.

9

8

5

COURT LN.

6

SUDBURY RD.

BEDFORD ST.

11

THOREAU ST.

2

LEXINGTON RD.

WALDEN ST.

12

CONCORD TURNPIKE   (RTE. 2)

3

{CONCORD}

T hough settled in 1635 as the first inland town in Massachusetts, charming Concord, sixteen miles northwest of Boston, first gained international repute in 1775. On the morning of April 19, patriot minutemen and militia fought off the British regulars on Concord's North Bridge—"the shot heard round the world" that marked the start of the American Revolution. By the middle of the nineteenth century, however, the grandchildren and great-grandchildren of those early patriots were ready to play a central role in

Nineteenth-century view of Concord by J. W. Barber

another revolution, albeit a quieter and gentler one. This rebellion involved the worlds of literature and ideas, and spawned two generations of intellectuals committed to social reform, spiritual uplift, and literary innovation.

Today you can still visit the beautifully maintained homes, studies, woods, and ponds—and bask in the warmth of the historic village—that once attracted some of the nineteenth century's greatest writers and thinkers.

The role of **Ralph Waldo Emerson** (1803–1882) in particular cannot be overemphasized when discussing literary Concord. The man known as "Concord's First Citizen" and "the Sage of Concord" was actually born and raised in Boston. Still, Concord was clearly Emerson's ancestral—not to mention his spiritual—home. Peter Bulkeley, Emerson's grandfather seven generations back, arrived in 1635 to help found Concord and become its first minister.

Grandfather William Emerson was another family minister, who reportedly was involved in and later wrote about the revolutionary activities on the North Bridge in April 1775. His family observed the encounter between patriots and redcoats from the windows of The Old Manse, the home Reverend Emerson had built five years earlier.

Waldo—as his friends called Ralph Waldo Emerson—followed his family's traditional pattern of education. He attended Boston Latin School, Harvard College, and Harvard Divinity School, and was ordained as the minister of Boston's Second Church (Unitarian) in 1829. That church was descended from the First Church of Boston, where Increase and Cotton Mather held forth during colonial times.

By 1832, however, Emerson's life was in turmoil. His young wife, Ellen Louisa Tucker, had died after only seventeen months of marriage. At the same time, his emerging personal philosophy about God was already in conflict with the Unitarian position, leading him to resign from the Second Church—and ultimately from the ministry altogether. In December of that year, he sailed to Europe, where he met with eminent British men of letters such as Thomas Carlyle, William Wordsworth, and Samuel Taylor Coleridge.

Once back in Boston, Emerson embarked on a new life of lecturing, writing, and embracing dissident New Englanders like himself. He also began replacing traditional Christian doctrines with a new philosophy called transcendentalism. The old concept of God was replaced by the "Over-Soul," and each person was encouraged to listen to his or her own inner voice while seeking the balance and unity within nature.

By 1834, Emerson had moved to Concord, staying first at his family's home (later called The Old Manse by Hawthorne), then, by the following year, in a house he purchased on the Cambridge Turnpike. Emerson's house, now a museum owned by his descendants, still stands at the intersection of the old turnpike and Lexington Road.

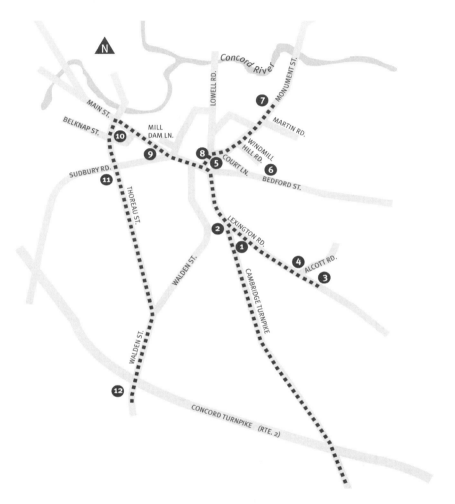

1. Concord Museum
2. Ralph Waldo Emerson house
3. The Wayside
4. Orchard House
5. Monument Square
   Civil War Memorial
   Concord Town House
6. Sleepy Hollow Cemetery
7. Monument Street
   The Old Manse
   North Bridge
8. Concord Town Center:
   Colonial Inn
   Masonic Lodge Building
   Site of the old Concord Jail
9. Concord Free Public Library
10. Thoreau-Alcott house
11. Concord Depot
12. Walden Pond State Reservation

Why did Emerson choose to make his home in Concord? In part because it was his ancestral home—but surely also because of the beautiful and tranquil natural landscape, still apparent today. As he noted in a *Journal* entry in 1846:

> *I think we escape something by living in the villages. In Concord here there is some milk of life, we are not so raving distracted with wind and dyspepsia. The mania takes a milder form. People go a-fishing, and know the taste of their meat. They cut their own whippletree in the woodlot, they know something practically of the sun and the east wind, of the under-pinning and the roofing of the house, of the pan and the mixture of the soils.*

In the course of his life here, Emerson's person, intellect, and home became beacons for a wealth of creative talent and literary genius from both near and far. Like Longfellow's home and Harvard College in Cambridge, or the Old Corner Bookstore and Elizabeth Peabody's Foreign Library and bookstore in Boston, the Emerson homestead served as a vital gathering place for the most fertile minds of mid-nineteenth-century America.

Emerson's friend and neighbor Louisa May Alcott, in an article for *The Youth's Companion*, described the aura and appeal of Emerson's home:

> *The marble walk that leads up to [Emerson's] door has been trodden by the feet of many pilgrims from all parts of the world, drawn thither by their love and reverence for him. In that famous study, his townspeople have had the privilege of seeing many of the great and good men and women of our time, and learning of their gracious host the finest lessons of true courtesy. I have often seen him turn from distinguished guests, to say a wise or kindly word to some humble worshipper sitting modestly in a corner, content merely to look and listen, and who went away to cherish that memorable moment long and gratefully.*

Ralph Waldo Emerson's study

WHAT WAS TRANSCENDENTALISM?

Transcendentalism combined religion, philosophy, mysticism, and ethics. Transcendentalists believed that:

- All living things were bound together;
- Humans were essentially good;
- Insight was more powerful than experience as a source of knowledge.

The birth of American transcendentalism dates from 1836, when a group of people—many of them Unitarian ministers—met in the Boston home of George Ripley to discuss German philosophy and social issues of the day. The Transcendental Club, as it was called, met periodically, with a fluid roster of members.

These men and women lived all over New England. They conversed by mail, as well as in meetings and private visits—most frequently in Boston and Concord.

—COURTESY OF THE CONCORD MUSEUM

Despite his love for Concord and the crowds that gathered around him there, Emerson was well known for hopping into horse-drawn coaches or onto cars of the Fitchburg Railroad (which ran along the course still followed by commuter trains today). He was also a popular lecturer who traveled widely to deliver his wisdom, interwoven with what Annie Fields called a "furtive humor." In his lifetime, Emerson gave close to fifteen hundred lectures, some nine hundred in Massachusetts alone.

The **Concord Museum**, at the intersection of Lexington Road and the Cambridge Turnpike, is the logical first stop on a visit to historic Concord. Founded in 1886 and based on a well-documented collection of Americana begun by Cummings Davis in the 1850s, it offers a visual encyclopedia of Concord's past.

A nationally significant collection of historical and literary artifacts, seventeenth- through nineteenth-century decorative arts galleries, and finely furnished period rooms featuring Concord clocks, furniture, and silver are only part of the museum's broad appeal. A film called *Exploring Concord* and engaging galleries that answer the frequent question *Why Concord?* help explain how the events in this small Massachusetts town had such a large impact on the world.

I like to be in your library when you are out of it. It seems a sacred place. I came here to find a book, that I might feel more life and be worthy to sleep, but there is so much soul here I do not need a book . . .

—MARGARET FULLER, LETTER TO RALPH WALDO EMERSON (1842)

Make much of your own place. The stars & celestial awning that overhang our simple Concord walks and discourses are as brave as those that were visible to Coleridge as he talked or to Dryden or Ben Jonson & Shakespeare or Chaucer & Petrarch & Boccaccio when they met.

—RALPH WALDO EMERSON, *JOURNAL* (1835)

In the self-guided *Why Concord?* exhibition, town history is introduced with the Algonkian natives and English settlers who lived with them in peace and "concord." The *Defending Concord* gallery focuses on the events that led to the start of the American Revolution in Lexington and Concord, including one of the original lanterns hung at the Old North Church the night of Paul Revere's "midnight ride."

Of course, the great nineteenth-century writers who brought together Boston, Cambridge, and Concord are given appropriate play. Two of Concord's leading figures—Ralph Waldo Emerson and Henry David Thoreau—enjoy prominent places at the museum.

Though best known for his sojourn at Walden Pond and the book that followed, Thoreau was also a naturalist, inventor, civil engineer, social critic, and philosopher. Among the many personal possessions in the Thoreau gallery are the desk Thoreau used when writing "Civil Disobedience" and *Walden*, the walking stick that he used on his excursions, a manuscript from his lyceum lecture notes (published as the essay "Walking"), the bedstead from his tiny house on Walden Pond, and pencils he improved at his family's pencil factory.

The entire study of transcendentalist philosopher, essayist, Unitarian minister, and popular lecturer Emerson is here as well. Arguably the most influential thinker of his time, this proponent of individualism and self-reliance greeted a constant stream of visitors in this book-lined room while assembling such works as his *Essays* and *Poems*. The furnishings here were moved from the **Emerson House,** diagonally across the street, when the museum was built on part of the Emerson apple orchard in 1930.

At the corner, bear right off the Cambridge Turnpike onto Lexington Road. This is part of the Battle Road of American Revolutionary fame. Running parallel to it for almost a mile, stretching behind some beautiful old homes, is the heavily wooded **Revolutionary Ridge**.

It's interesting to note that the writers in Concord who were part of America's nineteenth-century literary revolution were also attuned to the political revolution of the previous century. Many of them wrote stories or poems based on America's War for Independence, such as Hawthorne's *Septimius Felton*, Louisa May Alcott's *Tabby's Tablecloth*, and Emerson's "Concord Hymn." Meanwhile, the Revolution provided literary inspiration for their friends in Boston and Cambridge as well, most notably "Paul Revere's Ride" (1863) by Longfellow:

> *Listen, my children, and you shall hear,*
> *Of the midnight ride of Paul Revere,*
> *On the eighteenth of April, in Seventy-five;*
> *Hardly a man is now alive*
> *Who remembers that famous day and year.*

Farther down the street, at 455 Lexington Road, is **The Wayside**. (A parking lot across the way allows visits to both The Wayside and Orchard House.) The quaint Wayside is known as the only National Historic Landmark to have been the home of three literary families—those of Nathaniel Hawthorne, Louisa May Alcott, and Harriett Lothrop. Well over three hundred years old, it was also the first literary site to become part of the National Park Service.

Nathaniel Hawthorne (1804–1864) was descended from one of New England's oldest families. The Hathornes—as the name was originally spelled—were legislators, magistrates, soldiers, and sailors long associated with the town of Salem, northeast of Boston. One particular ancestor, Judge John Hathorne, participated in the Salem witch trials of 1692—a source of guilt that affected young Nathaniel and surely influenced his works, including *The House of Seven Gables* and *The Scarlet Letter*.

Nathaniel Hawthorne, 1846 crayon and chalk drawing by Eastman Johnson

It was perhaps a telling sign that Hawthorne was born on July 4, 1804—the twenty-eighth anniversary of America's independence. In his teen years, he declared his own independence from his family's past by deciding to become a writer. His seafaring father had died when the boy was just four, giving him a tendency toward solitude, somberness, and shy reserve that stayed with him throughout his life. An impressionable year of quiet near a favorite Maine lake was followed by his years at Bowdoin College, where he was a schoolmate of Longfellow and Franklin Pierce, the future U.S. president, who became a lifelong friend.

In the dozen years before publishing *The Scarlet Letter* (1850), Hawthorne spent several months in the experimental commune at Brook Farm (West Roxbury), married Sophia Peabody of Salem (the sister of Elizabeth Palmer Peabody), worked at the custom house in both Salem and Boston, and lived in The Old Manse in Concord, collecting the stories that became *Mosses from an Old Manse* (1846). The success of *The Scarlet Letter* allowed Nathaniel and Sophia to spend 1850–1851 in Lenox, in the beautiful Berkshire Mountains of western Massachusetts. It was an especially prolific period for him; in 1851 he produced three books: *The House of the Seven Gables, The Snow Image and Other Twice-Told Tales,* and *A Wonder-Book for Girls and Boys,* and began a friendship with Herman Melville, who revered Hawthorne and dedicated his masterpiece, *Moby-Dick* (also 1851) to him.

In 1852, the family returned to Concord and settled into The Wayside, the only home that Hawthorne ever owned. Before he called it "Wayside," the Alcotts had named it "Hillside" when they owned it from 1845 to 1852. Many of the childhood events Louisa described in *Little Women,* including her amateur plays, occurred at Hillside. As it happened, The Wayside was saved by a later owner, **Harriett Mulford Stone Lothrop** (1844–1924), who made her own literary reputation as **Margaret Sidney**, creator of the *Five Little Peppers* children's books.

UTOPIAN COMMUNITIES

During the nineteenth century, idealized agrarian communes were created as experimental sites for cooperative living. Their goals included developing socially progressive thought—like socialism and transcendentalism —and implementing their principles in everyday life. In the Greater Boston area, the best-known communities were George Ripley's Brook Farm in West Roxbury and Bronson Alcott's New Eden at Fruitlands, in the town of Harvard.

Like founder George Ripley, a large number of the participants in **Brook Farm Institute of Agriculture and Education** (1841-1847) were past or present members of the Unitarian Church who had come to espouse transcendentalist philosophies. Many of the area's most fertile minds—from Nathaniel Hawthorne, John Sullivan Dwight, and Charles Dana to Ralph Waldo Emerson, Margaret Fuller, and Horace Greeley— were either members of or visitors to George and Sophia Ripley's renowned community. Though the intellectual life there was vibrant and the school excellent, economics played a major part in Brook Farm's demise: these thinkers were not skilled farmers, and the soil was inadequate for good crop growth.

Far shorter-lived than Brook Farm was the **New Eden at Fruitlands,** founded by Bronson Alcott and Charles Lane in 1843 and ended later that winter. A brilliant but impractical transcendentalist, Alcott moved his wife and daughters to Fruitlands to share in farming the land, communing with nature, and engaging in intellectual exchanges. As it turned out, Bronson's wife, Abigail May, was left with the impossible task of holding the physical ship together as Bronson and his handful of fellow thinkers—including, at times, Thoreau and Emerson—spent more hours sailing on philosophical waters.

Though its site is listed on the National Register of Historic Places, no park or museum commemorates Brook Farm, located at 670 Baker Street, West Roxbury. Nathaniel Hawthorne incorporated his experiences at Brook Farm in describing the fictional Blithedale of his *Blithedale Romance* (1852).

Fruitlands, at 102 Prospect Hill Road in Harvard, is still a delightful place to visit. Purchased and saved by author and preservationist **Clara Endicott Sears** (1863–1960), the scenic, rolling hillsides here were opened to the public in 1914 and evolved into what is now known as the Fruitlands Museums. In addition to Bronson Alcott's old farmhouse—which contains some interesting transcendentalist memorabilia—guests can enjoy a Shaker Museum, an Indian Museum, a Picture Gallery featuring landscapes from the Hudson River School and early folk art portraits, as well as a tea room, picnic space, and nature trails.

The main structure of The Wayside is a colonial farmhouse, although each literary family made its own distinctive additions. The east chamber, for example, is colonial, but Bronson Alcott added wings and porches, among other things. The unique three-story tower was added by Hawthorne; his study on its top floor still holds his writing desk, murals painted in tribute to him, and his bookcases. Other interesting exhibits are shown in the adjacent barn.

James T. Fields, in *Yesterdays with Authors* (1871), mused on Hawthorne's life at The Wayside:

I saw him frequently at the Wayside, in Concord. He now seemed happily in the dwelling he had put in order for the calm and comfort of his middle and later life. He had added a tower to his house, in which he could be safe from intrusion, and where he could muse and write. Never was a poet or romancer more fitly shrined. . . . Shut up in his tower, he could escape from the tumult of life, and be alone with only the birds and the bees in concert outside his casement.

Hawthorne himself was a little more dubious about the dwelling he had "put in order," as amusingly recalled in his *Letters*:

I have been equally unsuccessful in my architectural projects; and have transformed a simple and small old farm-house into the absurdest anomaly you ever saw; but I really was not so much to blame here as the village-carpenter, who took matters into his own hands, and produced an unimaginable sort of thing instead of what I asked for. . . . I was given over to Satan, surely, when I first had to do with carpenters and painters.

The house most closely associated with *Little Women* is **Orchard House**, at 399 Lexington Road, a short walk from The Wayside. In 1857 it was purchased by **Amos Bronson Alcott** (1799–1888), one of the most brilliant and unworldly of all the Concord transcendentalists. A great philosopher and teacher, sincere utopian, and decidedly impractical visionary, Alcott was considered a singularly excellent man. "It is impossible to quarrel with [Bronson Alcott]," observed Hawthorne, "for he would take all your harsh words like a saint."

The self-taught son of a Connecticut farmer, Alcott moved to Boston in 1828 and married Abigail May two years later. Blending

INDEPENDENCE DAY

The Fourth of July seems to have taken on a special significance in the literary and sociopolitical history of Greater Boston. Nathaniel Hawthorne, for example, was born on Independence Day in 1804. July 4, 1829, was the day William Lloyd Garrison made his first antislavery speech at the Park Street Church in Boston; three years later, at the same spot, the song "America" made its debut. It was on Independence Day, 1837, that Ralph Waldo Emerson's "Concord Hymn" was first sung at the completion of the Battle Monument next to the North Bridge. On Independence Day in 1845, Henry David Thoreau moved into his house on Emerson's land by Walden Pond.

In September 1837, Emerson delivered an address at Harvard College that came to be called America's "*intellectual* Declaration of Independence." In this "American Scholar" speech, he noted:

> The scholar is the delegated intellect. In the right state he is Man Thinking. . . . Meek young men grow up in libraries, believing it their duty to accept the views which Cicero, which Locke, which Bacon have given, forgetful that Cicero, Locke and Bacon were only young men in libraries when they wrote these books.

In 1975, the Pulitzer Prize–winning poet Archibald MacLeish published *The Great American Fourth of July Parade*, which imagined Presidents John Adams and Thomas Jefferson commenting on the State of the Union in the 1970s. Adams —who, with his wife, Abigail, lived in Boston as well as Quincy—corresponded with Jefferson for many years and was a close friend. In 1813 Adams wrote: "You and I ought not to die, before we have explained ourselves to each other." Thirteen years later —on July 4, 1826, the fiftieth anniversary of the Declaration of Independence they had created together—Jefferson and Adams both died, each unaware of the other's demise.

romantic ideals about the goodness of mankind with progressive educational thought, he set up a series of schools in Connecticut, Pennsylvania, and Massachusetts. Among his experiments were the Temple School in Boston, the utopian community at Fruitlands in Harvard, Massachusetts, and the Concord School of Philosophy—the last, a pioneering summer school for adult education and his most successful school. Though Alcott was for many years short of cash, he was able to buy Orchard House for his wife and their daughters Anna,

Bronson Alcott

Louisa, Elizabeth, and May, with a little help from some devoted relatives and friends. From 1880 until shortly before his death, he ran the School of Philosophy from the "Hillside Chapel" behind the house.

The main house was created from one seventeenth- and one eighteenth-century structure which Alcott joined, improved, and vigorously landscaped. Writer Lydia Maria Child, after first visiting Orchard House, was impressed with its architectural integrity and unique renovations. In a letter to Mrs. S. B. Shaw in 1876, Child wrote:

The house of the Alcotts took my fancy greatly. . . . Mr. Alcott has an architectural taste more intelligible than his Orphic sayings. He let every old rafter and beam stay in its place, changed old ovens and ash-holes into Saxon-arched alcoves, and added a wash-woman's old shanty to the rear. The result is a house full of queer nooks and corners, and all manner of juttings in and out. It seems as if the spirit of some old architect had brought it from the Middle Ages and dropped it down in Concord.

Still, it was not Bronson but his daughter **Louisa May Alcott** (1832–1888) who brought everlasting fame to Orchard House. Born in Germantown, Pennsylvania, Louisa was an independent spirit. Though she held a variety of jobs in those early years—including teacher, domestic servant, and Civil War nurse—writing was clearly her passion.

In 1852, under the pen name of Flora Fairfield, she published her first story, "The Rival Painters," in Boston's *Olive Branch*. In 1854, James T. Fields of the Old Corner Bookstore read her essay "How I Went Out to Service" and informed her to "Stick to teaching, Miss Alcott. You can't write." Nevertheless, Louisa persisted, constantly writing in a number of genres—from poetry and theatrical drama to love stories and gothic tales. Her short pieces were soon followed by books, including *Flower Fables* (1854)—written for Emerson's daughter

Ellen and inspired by walks with Thoreau—and *Hospital Sketches* (1863), which described her nursing experiences during the Civil War.

It was here in Orchard House that Louisa wrote many of her short stories for periodicals, including the *Atlantic Monthly* and popular "juveniles." Yet the house will always be remembered as the fictional setting for *Little Women* (1868), her blockbuster novel that cast the four Alcott sisters as the four March sisters—Louisa herself became Jo March, Anna became Meg, Elizabeth became Beth, and May became Amy—and their mother as "Marmee" in the retelling of many family experiences. Orchard House is also where Louisa actually wrote *Little Women*:

"Jo! Jo, where are you?" cried Meg, at the foot of the garret stairs.

"Here!!" answered a husky voice from above; and, running up, Meg found her sister eating apples and crying over the Heir of Redclyffe, *wrapped up in a comforter on an old three-legged sofa by the sunny window. This was Jo's favorite refuge; and here she loved to retire with a half a dozen russets and a nice book to enjoy the quiet and the society of a pet rat who lived near by, and didn't mind her a particle.*

Visitors to Orchard House will recognize and appreciate many rooms, objects, and the aura described in *Little Women*, including bedchambers, kitchen, study, and parlor, as well as May Alcott's drawings on her walls, a trunk of theatrical costumes, and Louisa's half-moon desk and inkwell. The dining room looks much as it did when the Alcotts and their guests, many of them writers and intellectuals, were entertained here by music, theater, and good conversation.

It's interesting to note that many of the March family adventures did not actually take place here at Orchard House, for Alcott liberally incorporated segments of many of

Louisa May Alcott, circa 1858

Gish Jen on Louisa May Alcott and Ralph Waldo Emerson

I was Jo March, of course—writing away, cutting my hair, ever so gently refusing rich Teddy. Is there a woman writer in America who would not say so? How she loved Marmee, and indulged Amy, but chose for herself the most unglamorous Professor Bhaer? And who would not return, if she could, to the clear-cut world of the March family, worldly privations and all—to that warmth and nobility and simplicity?

I suspect I took the pen name Gish Jen in part because it sounded like Jo March—an androgynous spondee that spoke of independence. I invented myself in her image, and if one day I had to leave her and her author behind—if I had to progress beyond *Pilgrim's Progress*, and "drying tears and bearing burdens"—it was not without a heartache much like that with which Jo left her first family and first self.

As for where I ventured—that was first of all down the street to tangle, like Margaret Fuller, with Emerson. Was there ever a thinker more at odds with Confucius? Self-reliance! What an idea. For anyone Emerson threatens to burn down the house; for this nice Chinese girl he seemed to torch the whole countryside. And yet his call, not only for a new literature, but for a literature endlessly new, for writers who write not only against the past but against their own best inventions—that seemed a call I could hear. There was room in his program for me, for anyone; anyone could be an American writer, she only had to find her power, then find it again; to name herself Man Thinking.

Emerson was the first subversive, and still inspires every serious writer. The goal is still to gather up our times' rejected thoughts, and to return them, if we can, with a certain alienated majesty.

her former homes into *Little Women*. (In the course of their marriage, her parents lived in more than twenty different places!) In fact, many of the childhood events she describes occurred at the Alcotts' former home Hillside—the house Hawthorne called Wayside—right next door.

Little Women, first edition frontispiece, 1868, with illustration by May Alcott

Though Louisa and her father have garnered the most attention over the years, every member of the family was interested in writing and had their own special talents: Mrs. Alcott was considered by many to have been the best writer in the family, and was an abolitionist and one of Boston's first social workers; Anna was particularly fond of acting and, with Louisa, helped start the Concord Dramatic Union; Elizabeth was a musician, but died when she was only twenty-two; and May was a professional artist and teacher who mentored young Daniel Chester French, though her career was ended by her untimely death at age thirty-nine.

Sculptor French later remembered the Alcotts and their home in Caroline Ticknor's *May Alcott, A Memoir* (1927):

I was always included . . . in the frequent invitations to supper or evening gatherings [at Orchard House] where there were literary games of charades or only conversation. Serene and courtly, his long silver locks curling about his neck, his fresh pink and white complexion set off by an expanse of snowy linen with white cravat, Mr. Alcott had much the aspect of an old portrait. He looked on at our diversions as from a loftier sphere, occasionally joining in the conversation or smiling approvingly at the humor of it, while the dear old lady who had not only been his helpmeet, but also a mainstay to the erratic genius through the many anxious years before the talented Louisa came so gallantly to the rescue, lent to the conversation her sweet reasonableness and her ever-quick response. The daughters, however, were most in evidence, as their elders seemed to wish. Miss Louisa's nimble wit and Miss May's gayety were sure to make material for diversion. One felt here that indeed "people were of more importance than things."

In the same memoir, French fondly remembered May Alcott as his first art mentor:

> *I may be able to record the peculiar debt I owe her in introducing me to the potentialities of sculpture. I had been whittling and carving things from wood and gypsum, and even from turnips, as many boys do, and, as usual, "the family" thought the product remarkable. My father spoke about them to Miss Alcott, as the artist of the community, and she, with her ever-ready enthusiasm, immediately offered to give me her modeling clay and tools. . . . I still [half a century later] have one of the modeling tools she gave me.*

Like The Wayside, Orchard House was preserved at the turn of the twentieth century by **Margaret Sidney**—the pen name of **Harriett Mulford Stone Lothrop** (1844–1924)—who promoted the cause of historic preservation in Concord. In addition to saving Orchard House and The Wayside, she preserved the Grapevine Cottage (the home of the famed Concord grape) and the Old Tolman House on Monument Square. Though she wrote books on Concord's rich history, Lothrop was best remembered for her popular adventures of a family of five mischievous siblings known as "the Little Peppers." The best-known volume of this children's series, *Five Little Peppers and How They Grew* (1881), sold more than 2 million copies in its first fifty years.

Drive back on Lexington Road toward the center of Concord. On the right you'll see the beautiful home of the **Concord Art Association**, which was once used as a safe house for escaped slaves on the Underground Railroad.

On the left, the First Parish Church stands on the site of the Provincial Congress meetings of 1774–1775, which resolved to stockpile military supplies in Concord and raise companies of minutemen in the neighboring villages. Just beyond the church is the old **Wright Tavern**, where British regulars assembled in April 1775 before proceeding to the North Bridge.

Bear to the right, passing through **Monument Square** and past the town's prominent Civil War memorial. (When the memorial was dedicated in 1867, Ralph Waldo Emerson was asked to give the speech.) Across the street is the **Concord Town House**, which served not only as town hall but also as a popular lecture hall and rallying point for writers, abolitionists, and other prominent figures in the nineteenth century, from Emerson, Thoreau, and Bronson Alcott to William Lloyd Garrison, Wendell Phillips, and John Brown.

In April 1875, President Ulysses S. Grant and other government officials commemorated the centennial of the Revolution in Concord. A group of women gathered here, at the Town House, awaiting the escort that had been promised them to the festivities at the North Bridge. Curiously, no one came. Louisa May Alcott remembered the ladies' furor later that year in an article for the *Woman's Journal*:

> *Patience has its limits, and . . . when some impetuous soul cried out "Come on and let us take care of ourselves" . . . skirts were kilted up, arms locked, and with one accord, the light brigade charged over the red bridge, up the hill, into the tented field, rosy and red-nosed, dishevelled but dauntless. . . . [Be warned that the] tax-paying women of Concord, will not be left to wait uncalled upon . . . and, following in the footsteps of their forefathers, will utter another protest that shall be heard "round the world."*

It's probably no surprise that in 1880, Louisa, an ardent supporter of woman's suffrage, became the first woman to vote here in a local school election.

Sleepy Hollow Cemetery:
A Walking Tour
Approximate Time: 45–60 Minutes

Turn right just before Town Hall onto Route 62 East. The winding country road—a mere three-tenths of a mile from Town Hall—leads to the main entrance of **Sleepy Hollow Cemetery**, which shares its name with Washington Irving's popular novel.

Following in the innovative footsteps of Mount Auburn Cemetery (1831) in Cambridge, Sleepy Hollow was designed by Horace William Shalet Cleveland and Robert Morris Copeland as a beautifully landscaped rural garden cemetery. As at Mount Auburn, the land was already a popular wooded walking place frequented by Hawthorne, Fuller, Emerson, and their friends. Interestingly, Henry David Thoreau was hired to survey Sleepy Hollow's pond and the road leading to the front gate. And it was Ralph Waldo Emerson—Concord's acknowledged spiritual center and perennial orator of choice—who gave the address at the cemetery's formal consecration in 1855.

"Shadows haunt these groves," Emerson observed in his speech. "All that ever lived about them clings to them. . . . And when these acorns that are falling at our feet are oaks overshadowing our children in a remote century, this mute green bank will be full of history."

The "mute green bank" filled with the most literary history at Sleepy Hollow is called **Authors' Ridge**, clearly marked by signs inside the cemetery. Nathaniel Hawthorne, Henry David Thoreau, Ralph Waldo Emerson, the Alcotts, and Margaret Sidney are interred on this hill. Elizabeth Palmer Peabody, of bookshop fame, is another resident; her gravesite is below Authors' Ridge.

In its earliest days, Sleepy Hollow was a relatively undiscovered gem—or so thought Nathaniel Hawthorne, as noted in his *Passages from the American Notebooks* (published in 1868, though the original passage was written in August 1842):

> *After leaving the book at Mr. Emerson's, I returned through the woods, and entering Sleepy Hollow, I perceived a lady reclining near the path*

which bends along its verge. It was Margaret [Fuller] herself. She had been there the whole afternoon, meditating or reading. . . . She said that nobody had broken her solitude, and was just giving utterance to a theory that no inhabitant of Concord ever visited Sleepy Hollow, when we saw a whole group of people entering the sacred precincts. . . .

In the midst of our talk we heard footsteps above us, on the high bank: and while the intruder was still hidden among the trees, he called to Margaret, of whom he had gotten a glimpse. Then he emerged from the green shade; and, behold, it was Mr. Emerson, who, in spite of his clerical consecration, had found no better way of spending the Sabbath than to ramble among the woods. He appeared to have had a pleasant time; for he said that there were Muses in the woods today, and whispers to be heard in the breezes.

The beloved **Hawthorne**, at the age of fifty-nine, was one of the first of his illustrious circle to die. He was buried at Sleepy Hollow in 1864, only nine years after it had been consecrated. James T. Fields remembered that bittersweet day in *Yesterdays with Authors* (1871):

On the 24th of May we carried Hawthorne through the blossoming orchards of Concord, and laid him down under a group of pines, on a hillside, overlooking historic fields. All the way from the village church to the grave the birds kept up a perpetual melody. The sun shone brightly, and the air was sweet and pleasant, as if death had never entered the world. Longfellow and Emerson, Channing and Hoar, Agassiz and Lowell, Greene and Whipple, Alcott and Clarke, Holmes and Hillard, and other friends whom he loved, walked slowly by his side that beautiful spring morning. The companion of his youth and his manhood, for whom he would willingly, at any time, have given up his own life, Franklin Pierce, was there among the rest, and scattered flowers into the grave. The unfinished Romance, which had cost him so much anxiety, the last literary work on which he had ever been engaged, was laid on his coffin.

Not surprisingly, the Literary Trail's omnipresent sculptor, **Daniel Chester French** (1850–1931), has a major piece at Sleepy Hollow. The moving Melvin Memorial (1906–1908) honors three brothers—Asa, John, and Samuel Melvin—all of whom joined the First Massachusetts Heavy Artillery,

Company K, and were killed in the Civil War. Like the Milmore Memorial, which French created for two brothers at Forest Hills Cemetery, the Melvin features a majestic female angel draped in a shroud and holding a bouquet. While Forest Hills's *Death and the Sculptor* shows the maternal, loving angel of death facing the artist while gently stopping his hand, the Melvin angel faces forward, sensually peering out from beneath a draped American flag. And while the former is cast in bronze, the latter is a marble rendering.

Though French was born in Exeter, New Hampshire, his family moved to Cambridge, Massachusetts, before settling permanently in Concord. His mother reportedly noticed little "Dan's" potential as a sculptor when the child began making comic characters from her turnips. Since Boston had no school of sculpture at the time, Dan picked up some principles of art from May Alcott, who had returned from her art studies in Paris. Other early inspiration came from William Morris Hunt, John Quincy Adams Ward, and William Rimmer.

Daniel Chester French,
Minute Man

French's break came through his friend Ralph Waldo Emerson, who helped him win his first major commission; the *Minute Man* was unveiled for the centennial celebration at the North Bridge in Concord on April 19, 1875. After traveling in Europe, gathering knowledge and inspiration from different studios, French returned to the United States, where he worked, studied, and developed his distinctive style.

By 1913, when he received the commission for the Lincoln Memorial in Washington, D.C., French was considered America's leading sculptor. He died in 1931, at Chesterwood, his summer studio in the Berkshire hills of western Massachusetts. He maintained a home and studio in Concord, now privately owned, throughout his life.

Return to Monument Street on Route 62 West. Turn right and follow the road down to the parking lot by the North Bridge.

The **Old Manse**, at 269 Monument Street, is another example of the intertwining revolutions in Concord. The Reverend William Emerson, a patriot minister, had the house built in 1770. He responded to and later wrote in his journal about the alarm of April 19, 1775, and the historic encounter on the adjacent North Bridge. Six decades later, his grandson Ralph Waldo Emerson began writing *Nature* from his second-floor study here, overlooking the site of the North Bridge. While boarding at The Old Manse, Emerson was asked to deliver an address on the bicentennial of the town of Concord. On September 11, 1835, flanked by elderly survivors of the North Bridge encounter, he delivered his "Historical Discourse," which borrowed from Grandfather Emerson's patriot journals.

The young Nathaniel Hawthorne and his wife, Sophia Peabody, spent what they claimed were the "three happiest years" of their lives, from 1842 through 1845, when they rented The Old Manse. Of the seventeen short stories Hawthorne wrote here, sixteen were published in *Mosses from an Old Manse*, in which he immortalized this beloved home:

> *How gently, too, did the sight of the Old Manse—best seen from the river, overshadowed with its willows, and all environed about with the foliage of its orchard and avenue—how gently did its gray, homely aspect rebuke the spectacular extravagances of the day!*

The house was actually called a variety of names for its first eighty-four years. It was Hawthorne who formally "christened" the structure with the publication of *Mosses from an Old Manse*. The word *manse* means the

The Old Manse, Concord, circa 1885

house of a clergyman, or a parsonage, and alluded to its first inhabitant, the Reverend William Emerson.

Visitors to The Old Manse can see the original structure and its minor additions as well as the vegetable garden—cultivated since the eighteenth century and planted in 1842 by Thoreau as a wedding gift for the Hawthornes. The dining room window and the north window of the upstairs study bear a number of inscriptions from this time, etched with Sophia's diamond wedding ring. Hawthorne and Emerson's study—where, typically, Hawthorne faced in and Emerson faced out—is a revered site. So too is the Concord River, which flows behind The Old Manse, and which many an author delighted to describe.

Hawthorne, for example, mused on the river's peace and pace in *Mosses from an Old Manse*:

> *It may well be called the Concord, the river of peace and quietness; for it is certainly the most unexcitable and sluggish stream that ever loitered imperceptibly towards its eternity—the sea.*

Thoreau made a similar observation in *A Week on the Concord and Merrimack Rivers*:

> *[The] Concord River is remarkable for the gentleness of its current, which is scarcely perceptible, and some have referred to its influence on the proverbial moderation of the inhabitants of Concord, as exhibited in the Revolution and on later occasions. It has been proposed that the town should adopt for its coat of arms a field verdant, with the Concord circling nine times round. I have read the descent of an eighth of an inch in a mile is sufficient to produce a flow. Our river has, probably, very near the smallest allowance.*

You can see the serenely sluggish Concord River by walking past The Old Manse toward the **North Bridge**.

Though commonly called the *Old* North Bridge—even on the sign in the Monument Street parking lot—this movingly rustic bridge was actually erected by the state of Massachusetts in 1956, replacing three other commemorative versions from 1875, 1889, and 1909. (In 2004, the 1956 bridge underwent a major restoration by the National Park Service.)

The truly "old" North Bridge, where the "shots heard 'round the world" were fired in 1775, was deliberately dismantled by the town of Concord in 1793. Though romantic versions of the tale have the British regulars ripping up planks in anger and

North Bridge, Concord

feeble defense, the truth is substantially tamer. (Yes, they yanked off a few boards but came nowhere near destroying the bridge.) After years of discussion, Concord Town Meeting voted to remove the North Bridge because populations had shifted and roads had been realigned. So the obsolete North Bridge was replaced by a more conveniently located bridge a few hundred yards away. (The bridge, incidentally, was again placed at the original site for the centennial of the famed 1775 battle).

The bridge here today is still a breathtaking sight, probably closer to the design of the original bridge than any that preceded it. On the Monument Street side is the obelisk memorializing one of the opening battles of the American Revolution, dedicated on July 4, 1837. It was for this ceremony that Emerson wrote his "Concord Hymn."

Across the river is French's impressive bronze *Minute Man* on a seven-foot granite pedestal. Cast in the Ames Foundry in Chicopee, Massachusetts, the statue was made from ten Civil War cannon donated to the project by Congress. Inscribed with the "Concord Hymn," the statue was dedicated—along with the 1875 version of the North Bridge—in the centennial festivities of April 19, 1775:

By the rude bridge that arched the flood,
Their flag to April's breeze unfurled,
Here once the embattled farmers stood,
And fired the shot heard 'round the world.

Drive back to Concord Center and Monument Square on Monument Street. You'll pass the **Colonial Inn**, the right section of which was once the home of Thoreau's aunts and housed his entire family during Henry's last two years of study at Harvard. The Colonial Inn is still a popular gathering place and a perfect place to stop for afternoon tea and conversation.

The brick **Masonic Lodge Building** on the next corner was a school where Thoreau taught after his graduation from college. He soon resigned from the job, refusing to use corporal punishment for his students.

Bearing left around the square, the site of the old **Concord Jail** is on your right. In July 1846, Thoreau spent the night here for refusing to pay his federal taxes. His protest was heard often: he was withholding funds from a government that condoned slavery and that engaged in a war he did not support. This experience led to his writing "Civil Disobedience," which was initially prepared as a lecture in 1848, and first published by Elizabeth Peabody in 1849 under the title "Resistance to Civil Government."

Turn right onto Main Street. Wending your way through the center of town, you'll see streets and buildings that would still look familiar to the Alcotts, Emersons, Thoreaus, and their friends. Though the names and owners have changed, the basic layout, many of the buildings, and the aura have not. Fine places for literary browsing include bookshops, new and used, as well as the library.

Main Street leads you to one of the town's quietest gems. Established in 1873, the **Concord Free Public Library** is a fine and architecturally fascinating building that holds not only the town's circulating and reference collections, but also incredibly rich special collections documenting Concord history, life, landscape, literature, and people from 1635 to the modern day. The library offers world-famous manuscripts and archival records, extensive collections of photographs and ephemera, choice works of Concord-related art, and an astonishing number of books (including rare first editions) by Concord's resident authors, both past and present. In the library's rotunda is a seated statue of Emerson by Daniel Chester French—one of a number of examples of the sculptor's work in the library's art collection.

If you stay on Main Street, forking to the right of the library, you will pass Academy Lane on the left. This is the neighborhood where

> *I went to the woods because I wished to live*
> *deliberately, to front only the essential facts of life,*
> *and see if I could not learn what it had to teach, and not,*
> *when I came to die, discover that I had not lived.*

—HENRY DAVID THOREAU, *WALDEN* (1854)

Henry David Thoreau and his older brother, John, started their own coeducational high school, which existed for three years. The building was later moved and can now be seen at 25 Middle Street, the first right turn off Academy Lane.

Continue down Main Street toward the light at the intersection with Thoreau Street. Three houses before that light, on the left side of the street, is a yellow building numbered 255, the **Thoreau-Alcott house**. Thoreau lived here for the last dozen years of his life, from 1850 to 1862. In 1877, the year after America's Centennial celebration, Louisa May Alcott and her sister Anna bought this house. Their mother died here in 1877.

Turn left at the lights onto Thoreau Street, which you will follow to Route 2 and Walden Pond. Just after turning onto Thoreau, note Belknap Street on the right. It leads to the neighborhood called "Texas," where the Thoreaus lived while Henry was at Walden Pond. He used to walk on the railroad tracks here, since they provided the most direct route between this site and his Walden house.

As you continue on Thoreau Street, on the right you'll pass the old **Concord Depot** for the Fitchburg Railroad. The commuter rail from Boston makes regular stops here, as have thousands of trains since the Golden Age of American literature. The Fitchburg Railroad first stopped in Concord in June of 1844. Without it, Emerson and his peers might have traveled far less frequently from Concord to Boston—and thereby been far less present at Ticknor & Fields, the Boston Athenaeum, Saturday Club meetings at the Parker House, and other favorite haunts.

In May 1873, the depot was the site of one particularly poignant and spectacular event. A year earlier, the Emerson home had been ruined by a major fire, forcing the family to travel to Europe and Egypt while the house underwent repair. On their return in 1873, the Emersons' train was greeted at the depot by an assemblage of

Concord's finest citizens and a brass band playing "Home Sweet Home."

Then, as ever, Emerson appreciated his depot and train, and the freedom they allowed. As he noted in "Culture," from *The Conduct of Life* (1860):

> [T]he aesthetic value of railroads is to unite the advantages of town and country life, neither of which we can spare. A man should live in or near a large town. . . . In town he can find . . . opera, theater and panorama; the chemist's shop, the museum of natural history; the gallery of fine arts; the national orators, in their turn. . . . In the country he can find solitude and reading, manly labor, cheap living and his old shoes.

After crossing Route 2, you'll find yourself on Walden Street (Route 126). Not far down the road is a large parking lot on your left. Leave your car here, then cross the road to the main entrance of Walden Pond.

A favorite recreational, beach, and picnic area for more than a century, **Walden Pond State Reservation** is also a major literary shrine. Here **Henry David Thoreau** (1817–1862) built his ten-by-fifteen-foot hand-hewn house in 1845, as a place to escape the bustling outside world, to confront himself, and to "live deliberately." He also needed to recover from the loss of his beloved brother John, who had died in his arms three years earlier from an accidental straight-edge razor cut that caused tetanus.

Henry David Thoreau's house on the title page of *Walden* (1854)

Henry David Thoreau was twenty-eight years old when he began his two years, two months, and two days at Walden, reading, writing, walking, and thinking in Spartan semi-solitude. Like his friend and mentor Ralph Waldo Emerson, who loaned him the land for the tiny home, Thoreau believed the idealist transcendental philosophy that studying nature and knowing oneself

Jane Langton on
"The Importance of Whiskers"

One of our librarian aunts must have given us a set of Authors cards. The suits were not hearts and diamonds, spades and clubs, but Ralph Waldo Emerson (no facial hair, gentle smile), Oliver Wendell Holmes (side-whiskers), Nathaniel Hawthorne (handlebar mustache), John Greenleaf Whittier (chin-whiskers), James Russell Lowell (short hair, bushy mustache, and whiskers), Henry Wadsworth Longfellow (the works).

It was a boring-looking set of cards. We didn't care. It was just a game, played cross-legged on the floor. My brother would ask for *The Autocrat of the Breakfast Table*, hoping to round out his Holmes suit, my sister wanted *The Village Blacksmith* to complete her set of Longfellow.

But—how extraordinary it seems now—Henry Thoreau was not part of the game. I suppose at that time he wasn't thought worthy of such select company. Now, of course, he has transcended all the rest.

It wasn't till many years later that those tiresome-looking old men became interesting to me, especially since they were so profoundly imbedded in the local landscape. Well, they're every-where, these august presences. Their clever faces, their works, their Olympian friendships, all of these things provide a dense thicket for a mystery writer to wander in. Somehow they fatten and enrich a meagre plot.

Today I can't cross Boston Common without thinking of Emerson walking there with Walt Whitman—nor can I walk up Tremont Street without remembering the Saturday Club at the Parker House. I wish I knew in which Cambridgeport house Emily Dickinson spent many a homesick month while consulting a doctor about her eyes. Nor is it possible to find on Charles Street the house of publisher James Fields, where Dickens was an ailing guest in 1868, and where Annie Fields lived in a "Boston marriage" with Sarah Orne Jewett after her husband's death. Have you ever felt something tickle your cheek as you walk down Brattle Street? I'll tell you what it is—it's the ghostly whiskers of some long-dead transcendentalist.

were one and the same. "We must learn to reawaken and keep ourselves awake . . . by an infinite expectation of the dawn," he later noted in *Walden* (1854).

Both Emerson and Thoreau believed that the Self, as the source of the Divine, could perceive the Divine in the rest of the world. Thoreau was a thinker ahead of his time on many other issues as well. He decried class pretensions and corporal punishment of schoolchildren, for example, and doubted the benefits of succumbing to the world of business and material accumulation. Most often, Thoreau is admired today as a pioneer in passive resistance and wilderness preservation, and an inspiration to an impressive entourage that includes Mahatma Gandhi, Martin Luther King, Jr., Leo Tolstoy, and environmentalist John Muir.

Despite legends to the contrary, Thoreau was not a hermit during his stay at Walden. He welcomed visitors, walked into the center of Concord—a surprisingly easy jaunt—and earned money surveying, selling vegetables to neighbors, and lecturing. Moreover, Thoreau wasn't the only writer inspired by these calm, wooded shores. Walden has proved a source of words, wisdom, and ideas for many Concord authors, both then and now.

Today you can leisurely walk to the isolated site of Thoreau's house and drop commemorative stones on the cairn that Bronson Alcott and Mary Adams began here in 1872. You can also visit a furnished replica of his home, conveniently placed in the parking lot (another replica stands outside the Concord Museum). The **Thoreau Society Shop at Walden Pond**, by the parking lot, is well worth a visit.

Though lovers of literature now generally associate Walden Pond with Thoreau, his contemporaries did not. Instead, the most famous man at Walden Pond in the 1840s was "Ice King" Frederic Tudor, whose international export company cut huge blocks of ice from the winter waters here, transported them to Boston ports via the

Fitchburg Railroad, then sailed them to countries with warmer climates in need of cooling.

Thoreau—who loved Indian philosophers and kept a Hindu text, the *Bhagavad Gita*, next to his bed—was thrilled that ice from Walden might well end up in India. Unlike Frederic Tudor, however, Thoreau achieved his most widespread fame a century after his own death—in the environmentally aware, socially conscious decade of the 1960s.

All things, of course, shall pass. So too did Thoreau's retreat by Walden Pond, which he ended in 1847. In *Walden*, he later observed:

> *Time is but the stream I go a-fishing in. I drink at it; but while I drink I see the sandy bottom and detect how shallow it is. Its thin current slides away, but eternity remains.*

Though his time there was over, the lessons he learned were indelible:

> *I learned this, at least, by my experiment: that if one advances confidently in the direction of his dreams, and endeavors to live the life which he has imagined, he will meet with a success unexpected in common hours.*

During the summer of 2004, the 150th anniversary of the publication of Thoreau's *Walden* inspired a wealth of lectures, tours, walks, and other special events in Concord. The anniversary was also commemorated in W. Barksdale Maynard's *Walden Pond: A History* (2004), a fine and detailed overview of the man, the historic literary environment, and the pond.

When you come to the end of this final leg of the Literary Trail, you'll return via Route 126 to Route 2. Take a right on Route 2 and follow it back to Cambridge, a drive of twenty to thirty minutes.

Afterthought

As much as Ralph Waldo Emerson loved Concord, Boston, and Cambridge—and reveled in his trips between them— he'd have to admit that they were lacking in one major area: cafés. The European tradition of leisurely sipping coffee in a cozy, congenial atmosphere had simply not come to America during his lifetime. As Emerson noted in his *Journal* (1864):

> *A town in Europe is a place where you can go into a café at a certain hour of every day, buy . . . a cup of coffee, for six sous, & at that price, have the company of the wits, scholars, & gentlemen fond of conversation. That is a cheap & excellent club, which finds & leaves all parties on a good mutual footing.*

More than a century after Emerson's death, Greater Boston has finally caught up with European café society. In fact, ending your visit in Harvard Square—with its numerous bookstores, cafés, and cozy clubs—is the perfect finale to a day of following the footsteps of America's literary giants.

Meanwhile, city and neighborhood newspapers (and related Web sites) in Cambridge, Boston, and Concord all include listings for literary events today—from book signings, author readings, lectures, and panel discussions to poetry readings, poetry slams, story swaps, and other special events.

While Greater Boston's book fairs, readings, signings, and related activities draw authors from around the nation and the world, these events frequently feature local literati as well. Our rich array of contributors to "Author! Author!"—Anne Bernays, Henry Louis Gates, Jr., Gish Jen, Justin Kaplan, Jane Langton, David McCullough, and Robert Pinsky—all live and work nearby. Although Patricia Smith has moved away, she, like the others, makes both formal and informal appearances in Boston. And the lively spirit of contributor Julia Child—who passed away in 2004—will always be a part of Cambridge and Boston.

Other nationally acclaimed writers in the area include the inimitable James Carroll (*Crusade; Constantine's Sword*), biographer Doris Kearns Goodwin (*Wait Till Next Year; No Ordinary Time*), historian Thomas O'Connor (*Bibles, Brahmins, and Bosses; Boston: A to Z*), and novelists Christopher Tilghman (*Mason's Retreat; Roads of the Heart*) and Arthur Golden (*Memoirs of a Geisha*). Among the best of the area's booming mystery-suspense writers is Linda Barnes (*Big Dig; Coyote*), a Boston University graduate who has written numerous novels featuring Carlotta Carlyle, a 6-foot, 1-inch redheaded Boston private eye.

Poet and playwright Derek Walcott (*Omeros; The Prodigal*) lives and teaches in the Greater Boston area, as does poet Seamus Heaney (*The Spirit Level; Opened Ground*), and novelists Tom Perrotta (*Election; Little Children*) and Ha Jin (*War Trash; The Bridegroom*). Other residents/teachers include novelist Margot Livesey (*Banishing Verona; Eva Moves the Furniture*), research psychiatrist Robert Coles (*Children of Crisis; The Spiritual Life of Children*), and Robert Brustein (*The Theatre of Revolt; The Siege of the Arts*), the founding director of the Yale Repertory and American Repertory theaters.

Alice Hoffman (*Blackbird House; The Probable Future*) is also a Greater Bostonian, as is Dennis Lehane (*Mystic River; Darkness, Take My Hand*), Stephen McCauley (*The Man of the House; The Object of My Affection*), Elizabeth McCracken (*Niagara Falls All Over Again; The Giant's House*), nature writer John Hanson Mitchell (*Walking Towards Walden; Ceremonial Time*), and Robert Parker, author of the celebrated Spenser detective series. Syndicated columnist Ellen Goodman (*Turning Points; I Know Just What You Mean*) is based in the Boston area, and columnist/author Susan Orlean (*The Orchid Thief; The Bullfighter Checks Her Makeup*) splits her time between here and New York. And while novelist John Updike (*Rabbit, Run; Bech: A Book*) makes his home in the northern suburbs of Boston, he has roots at Harvard.

Among the groups that support, showcase, and regularly assemble this wealth of contemporary area authors is PEN New England (Poets/Playwrights, Essayists, Editors, Novelists), one of five regional branches of International PEN, the only worldwide organization of writing professionals (www.pen.ne-org). In Concord, the annual

Concord Festival of Authors (www.concordchamberofcommerce.org) has proven a popular and prestigious celebration of modern writers, with readings, signings, panel discussions, and parties. Meanwhile, a gaggle of bookstores, libraries, historic sites, museums, clubs, and educational institutions throughout the Greater Boston area sponsor year-round events related to literature and literary history.

The Calendar section of the Thursday *Boston Globe* is arguably the best single resource for finding literary and historic activities in the area, which are listed by category and location. Check items under "Poetry and Prose," "Lectures," "Museums," and "Walks and Tours." The Ideas & Books section of the *Boston Sunday Globe* has "Bookings" of author appearances for the upcoming week, as well as local bestsellers and reviews (available online at www.boston.com/news/globe/living/books/). Many bookstores in Boston, Cambridge, and Concord also have bulletin boards and Web sites with notices of upcoming literary events. The Literary Trail itself can be accessed at www.lit-trail.org or www.bostondiscoveries.com.

Suggested Readings

Numerous biographies of the individuals mentioned in this guide-book are available in bookstores and libraries. Below are volumes, some in print and some not, that include tales, facts, and quotations by and about many members of Greater Boston's literary community.

Amory, Cleveland. *The Proper Bostonians*. New York: Dutton, 1947.

Bacon, Edwin M. *Literary Pilgrimages in New England*. New York: Silver Burdett, 1902.

Barksdale, Richard, and Keneth Kinnamon. *Black Writers of America: A Comprehensive Anthology*. New York: Macmillan, 1972.

Beatty, Noëlle Blackmer. *Literary Byways of Boston & Cambridge*. Washington, D.C.: Starrhill Press, 1991.

Brooks, Van Wyck. *The Flowering of New England*. New York: E. P. Dutton, 1936.

Corbett, William. *Literary New England: A History and Guide*. Boston: Faber and Faber, 1993.

Eastman, John. *Who Lived Where: A Biographical Guide to Homes and Museums*. New York: Bonanza Books, 1983.

Fields, Annie. *Authors and Friends*. Boston: Houghton Mifflin, 1897.

Fields, James T. *Yesterdays with Authors*. Boston: Houghton Mifflin, 1871.

Flagg, Mildred B. *Boston Authors: Now and Then*. Cambridge, Mass.: Dresser, Chapman & Grimes, 1966.

Hall, Donald. *The Oxford Book of American Literary Anecdotes*. New York: Oxford University Press, 1981.

History Project, The. *Improper Bostonians*. Boston: Beacon Press, 1998.

Howe, Helen. *The Gentle Americans*. New York: Harper & Row, 1965.

Howe, M. A. DeWolfe, ed. *Memories of a Hostess: A Chronicle of Eminent Friendships Drawn Chiefly from the Diaries of Mrs. James T. Fields*. Boston: Atlantic Monthly Press, 1922.

_____. *Who Lived Here? A Baker's Dozen of Historic New England Houses and Their Occupants*. New York: Bramhall House, 1952.

Howells, William Dean. *Literary Friends and Acquaintance*. New York: Harper & Brothers, 1900.

Jacobs, Donald M., ed. *Courage and Conscience: Black & White Abolitionism in Boston*. Bloomington: Indiana University Press for the Boston Athenaeum, 1993.

Kaledin, Eugenia. *Literary Boston: Boston 200 Broadside Series*. Boston: Boston 200, 1975.

Kaplan, Justin, ed. *Bartlett's Familiar Quotations, 17th ed*. Boston: Little, Brown, 2002.

Kaufman, Polly Welts, Bonnie Hurd Smith, et al. *Boston Women's Heritage Trail: Four Centuries of Boston Women*. Boston: Boston Women's Heritage Trail, 1999.

Linscott, Robert N., ed. *State of Mind: A Boston Reader*. New York: Farrar, Straus, 1948.

A Literary Guide to Boston and Environs: A Special Edition of Ginn High School English Notes. Boston: Ginn and Company, 1965.

O'Connell, Shaun. *Imagining Boston: A Literary Landscape* Boston: Beacon Press, 1990.

Petronella, Mary Melvin, ed., for the New England Chapter of the Victorian Society in America. *Victorian Boston Today: Twelve Walking Tours*. Boston: Northeastern University Press, 2004.

Swift, Lindsay. *Literary Landmarks of Boston*. Boston: Houghton Mifflin, 1903.

Tryon, Warren S. *Parnassus Corner: A Life of James T. Fields, Publisher to the Victorians*. Boston: Houghton Mifflin, 1963.

Wilson, Rufus Rockwell. *New England in Letters*. New York: A. Wessels, 1904.

Wilson, Susan. *Garden of Memories: A Guide to Historic Forest Hills*. Boston: Forest Hills Educational Trust, 1998.

———. *Sites and Insights: An Essential Guide to Historic Landmarks In and Around Boston*. Boston: Beacon Press, 2004.

Winslow, Helen M. *Literary Boston of To-Day*. Boston: L. C. Page, 1902.

Wolfe, Theodore F. *Literary Shrines: The Haunts of Some Famous American Authors*. Philadelphia: J. B. Lippincott, 1895.

Museums, Historic Sites, and Resources on the Literary Trail of Greater Boston

Below is a list of museums, other historic sites, and related resources open to the general public that are mentioned in The Literary Trail of Greater Boston. Every effort has been made to be sure this information is accurate at the time of publication.

BOSTON

Boston Athenaeum
10¹/₂ Beacon Street
617-227-0270
www.bostonathenaeum.org
Wheelchair accessible

Boston Common
Bounded by Tremont, Park, Beacon, Boylston, and Charles Streets
617-723-8144, Friends of the Public Garden and Common
617-635-4505, Boston Park Rangers
www.friendsofthepublicgarden.org
Open year-round, seasonal guided tours available, free admission
Wheelchair accessible

Boston Public Garden
Bounded by Charles, Beacon, Arlington, and Boylston Streets
617-723-8144, Friends of the Public Garden and Common
617-635-4505, Boston Park Rangers
www.friendsofthepublicgarden.org
Open year-round, seasonal guided tours available, free admission
Wheelchair accessible

Boston Public Library
700 Boylston Street
617-536-5400
www.bpl.org
Open year-round, guided tours available, free admission
Wheelchair accessible

Commonwealth Avenue Mall
Commonwealth Ave., from Arlington Street to Kenmore Square
617-723-8144, Friends of the Public Garden and Common
617-635-4505, Boston Park Rangers
www.friendsofthepublicgarden.org
Open year-round, seasonal guided tours available, free admission
Wheelchair accessible

Forest Hills Cemetery
95 Forest Hills Ave., Jamaica Plain
617-524-0128
www.foresthillstrust.org
Open year-round, free admission, some fees for special events and periodic guided walks
Wheelchair accessible

Gibson House
137 Beacon Street
617-267-6338
www.thegibsonhouse.org
Open year-round, admission fee
No wheelchair access

Granary Burying Ground
83–115 Tremont Street
617-635-4505, Boston Park Rangers
www.cityofboston.gov
Open year-round, free admission
Wheelchair accessible

King's Chapel
58 Tremont Street
617-227-2155
www.kings-chapel.org
Open year-round, free admission, fees may be charged for special events
Wheelchair accessible

King's Chapel Burying Ground
58 Tremont Street
617-635-4505, Boston Park Rangers
www.cityofboston.gov
Open year-round, free admission
Wheelchair accessible

Mary Baker Eddy Library for the Betterment of Humanity
200 Massachusetts Ave.
888-222-3711
www.marybakereddylibrary.org
Open year-round; some facilities free, some paid exhibits
Wheelchair accessible

Massachusetts Historical Society
(A research library open to the public)
1154 Boylston Street
617-536-1608
www.masshist.org
Library open year-round, free admission
Wheelchair accessible

Massachusetts State House
Beacon and Park Streets
617-727-3676, tours and information
www.sec.state.ma.us/trs
Open year-round, free admission
Reservations recommended
Wheelchair accessible

**Museum of Afro American History
Abiel Smith School
African Meeting House**
46 Joy Street
617-725-0022
www.afroammuseum.org
Open year-round, suggested donation
Wheelchair accessible

Nichols House Museum
55 Mount Vernon Street
617-227-6993
www.nicholshousemuseum.org
Open year-round, admission fee
No wheelchair access

**Old Corner Bookstore building
Historic Boston Incorporated**
3 School Street
617-227-4679
www.historicboston.org
Open year-round, free admission
Wheelchair accessible

Old South Meeting House
310 Washington Street
617-482-6439
www.oldsouthmeetinghouse.org
Open year-round, admission fee
Wheelchair accessible

Omni Parker House
60 School Street
617-227-8600
www.omnihotels.com
Open year-round, free admission
Wheelchair accessible

Park Street Church
One Park Street
617-523-3383
www.parkstreet.org
Open seasonally, free admission
Wheelchair accessible

Park Street MBTA Station
Corner of Park and Tremont Streets
617-222-3200, MBTA customer service
www.mbta.com
Open year-round, token or pass required
Wheelchair accessible

Tremont Temple
88 Tremont Street
617-523-7320
www.tremonttemple.com
Open year-round, free admission, fees may be charged for special performances
Wheelchair accessible

William Hickling Prescott House
55 Beacon Street
617-742-3190
www.nscda.org/ma/william_hickling_prescott_house.htm
Open seasonally, admission fee
No wheelchair access

CAMBRIDGE

The Cambridge Center for Adult Education
Located in a former home of Margaret Fuller and The Blacksmith House
42 and 56 Brattle Street
617-547-6789
www.ccae.org
Open year-round, fees charged for classes and special programs
Wheelchair accessible

Club Passim
47 Palmer Street
617-492-7679
www.passimcenter.org
Open year-round, admission fee
charged for performances
No wheelchair access

Harvard University
Harvard Events & Information Center
1350 Massachusetts Ave.
617-495-1573
www.news.harvard.edu
Open year-round, guided tours
available, free admission
Wheelchair access to Harvard Yard; call
for additional information

Longfellow National Historic Site
105 Brattle Street
617-876-4491
www.nps.gov/long
Open seasonally, admission fee
First floor wheelchair accessible

Mount Auburn Cemetery
580 Mount Auburn Street
617-547-7105
www.mountauburn.org
Open year-round, free admission, fees for
maps, special events, and guided walks
Mostly wheelchair accessible

CONCORD

Colonial Inn
48 Monument Square
978-369-9200
www.concordscolonialinn.com
Open year-round, free admission
Wheelchair accessible

Concord Chamber of Commerce
978-369-3120
www.concordchamberofcommerce.org

Concord Free Public Library
129 Main Street
978-318-3300
www.concordnet.org/library
Open year-round, free admission
Wheelchair accessible

Concord Museum
200 Lexington Road
978-369-9763
www.concordmuseum.org
Open year-round, admission fee
Wheelchair accessible

Concord Town House
Town government offices for Concord
22 Monument Square
978-318-3001
Open year-round, free admission
Wheelchair accessible

Ralph Waldo Emerson House
28 Cambridge Turnpike
978-369-2236
Open seasonally, admission fee
No wheelchair access

North Bridge Site
Minute Man National Historical Park
Monument Street
978-369-6993
www.nps.gov/mima
Open year-round, free admission
Wheelchair accessible

The Old Manse
269 Monument Street
978-369-3909
www.oldmanse.org
Open seasonally, admission fee
First-floor wheelchair accessible

Orchard House
399 Lexington Road
978-369-4118
www.louisamayalcott.org
Open year-round except for first two
weeks in January, admission fee
1st floor wheelchair accessible

Sleepy Hollow Cemetery
Bedford Street (Route 62)
Open year-round, free admission
Partly wheelchair accessible

Walden Pond State Reservation
915 Walden Street (Route 126)
978-369-3254
Gift shop, www.thoreausociety.org
www.mass.gov/dcr/parks/northeast/
wldn.htm
Open year-round, parking fee
Shop, bathrooms wheelchair accessible

The Wayside
455 Lexington Road
978-369-6993
www.nps.gov/mima/wayside
Open seasonally, admission fee
Visitor Center wheelchair accessible

TRAILS

Some of the following trails can be self-guided; in other cases, you can join a group tour. Call or visit their Web sites for further information.

Black Heritage Trail/Boston African American National Historic Site
46 Joy Street
617-742-5415
www.nps.gov/boaf

Boston By Foot
Literary Landmarks Tour
617-367-2345
www.bostonbyfoot.com

Boston by Sea: A Musical Cruise Through Boston's Past
Boston History Collaborative
617-350-0358
Mass. Bay Lines 617-542-8000
www.bostonbysea.org

Boston Family History Web Site
(Virtual tour of Boston's ethnic neighborhoods)
Boston History Collaborative
617-350-0358
www.BostonFamilyHistory.com

Boston History Collaborative
617-350-0358
www.bostondiscoveries.com

Boston Women's Heritage Trail
617-522-2872
www.bwht.org

Freedom Trail
Boston National Historical Park
617-242-5642
www.nps.gov/bost
Freedom Trail Foundation
617-357-8300
www.thefreedomtrail.org

Literary Trail of Greater Boston
Boston History Collaborative
617-350-0358
www.literarytrailofgreaterboston.org

OTHER SITES

Site of Brook Farm
(Interpretive signage at site)
670 Baker Street
West Roxbury, Massachusetts
Open year-round, free admission

Fruitlands Museums
102 Prospect Hill Road
Harvard, Massachusetts
978-456-3924
www.fruitlands.org
Open seasonally, admission fee
Partially wheelchair accessible, call for information

House of the Seven Gables
54 Turner Street
Salem, Massachusetts
978-744-0991
www.7gables.org
Open year-round except January 1–13, admission fee
First floor, grounds, and museum shop wheelchair accessible

John F. Kennedy Library and Museum
Columbia Point, Boston, Massachusetts
617-514-1600
www.jfklibrary.org
Open year-round, admission fee
Wheelchair accessible

PEN New England
(Poets/Playwrights, Essayists, Editors, Novelists)
www.pen-ne.org

The Sargent House Museum
(Judith Sargent Murray)
49 Middle Street
Gloucester, Massachusetts
978-281-2432
www.sargenthouse.org
Open seasonally, admission fee
No wheelchair access

John Greenleaf Whittier Birthplace
305 Whittier Road
Haverhill, Massachusetts
978-373-3979
www.johngreenleafwhittier.com
Open year-round, admission fee
No wheelchair access

Author! Author! Contributors

Anne Bernays is the author of *Growing Up Rich, Professor Romeo,* and six other novels. She is a coauthor of two books of nonfiction and many essays and book reviews. Long a teacher of writing, Bernays and her husband, Justin Kaplan, are the authors of *Back Then: Two Lives in 1950s New York.* Her novel *Trophy House* will be published in 2005.

Julia Child introduced millions of Americans to the art of French cooking with her lively television broadcasts and cookbooks. She settled in Cambridge, Massachusetts, shortly after the publication of her first cookbook, *Mastering the Art of French Cooking.* In the four subsequent decades, she won Emmy awards for her television programs, wrote ten best-selling cookbooks, and was awarded the Presidential Medal of Freedom. She retired to her native California in 2001, and passed away in 2004.

Henry Louis Gates, Jr., one of *Time* magazine's "25 Most Influential Americans," is the chair of Afro-American Studies and director of the W. E. B. Du Bois Institute at Harvard University. He has written several books of literary criticism and is the editor of anthologies, encyclopedias, and magazines on the black experience. His numerous awards include a grant from the MacArthur Foundation and election to the Academy of Arts and Letters.

Gish Jen has written three acclaimed novels, *Typical American, Mona in the Promised Land,* and *The Love Wife,* and a collection of stories, *Who's Irish?* A graduate of Harvard University and the Iowa Writers' Workshop, she has received support from the Lannan Foundation, the Guggenheim Foundation, the Radcliffe Institute for Advanced Study, and others. She lives in Cambridge, Massachusetts, with her husband and two children.

Justin Kaplan, general editor of the sixteenth and seventeenth editions of Bartlett's *Familiar Quotations,* is the author of several biographies, including the Pulitzer Prize–winning *Mr. Clemens and Mark Twain* as well as *The Language of Names* and *Back Then: Two Lives in 1950s New York* (the last two coauthored with his wife, Anne Bernays). He and Bernays live in Cambridge, Massachusetts.

Jane Langton has written eighteen suspense novels. Many of her narratives happen in New England's most sacred literary shrines. Her titles include *The Transcendental Murder, God in Concord, The Memorial Hall Murder,* and *The Escher Twist.* Her series of children's fantasies, "The Hall Family Chronicles," is set in transcendental Concord. She lives in Lincoln, Massachusetts.

David McCullough is well known to TV audiences as host of *Smithsonian World* and *The American Experience* and narrator of numerous documentaries. Twice winner of the Pulitzer Prize and the National Book Award, he has also received the Francis Parkman Prize (twice) and other honors. McCullough has written a number of histories, including *John Adams* and *Truman.* He and his wife, Rosalee Barnes McCullough, in West Tisbury, Massachusetts.

Robert Pinsky, the thirty-ninth Poet Laureate of the United States, has written numerous books of poetry and prose. He has also translated Dante's *Inferno* and has been the poetry editor of the Internet magazine *Slate*. Pinsky teaches in the graduate writing program at Boston University and lives with his wife, Ellen, in Cambridge, Massachusetts.

Patricia Smith, the author of three poetry volumes—*Close to Death, Life According to Motown,* and *Big Towns, Big Talk*—is a National Poetry Slam champion and featured poet on HBO's Def Poetry Jam. She also authored *Africans in America,* a companion book to the PBS documentary, and the children's book *Janna and the Kings.* A former Boston resident, she lives in Westchester Country, New York, with her husband, Bruce, an Associated Press editor, and her granddaughter, Mikaila.

Credits

The authors gratefully acknowledge permission to reproduce the following:

Copyrighted photographs by Susan Wilson: Boston Women's Memorial; Bronson Alcott's Study, Orchard House, Concord; African Meetinghouse.

Courtesy of Susan Wilson: Pi Alley.

Photograph by Ralph Turcotte: 54th Regiment Memorial.

Courtesy of the Boston Public Library Print Department: Henry Adams, E. E. Cummings, Charles Dickens, Benjamin Franklin, Robert Frost, Martin Luther King, Jr., Robert Lowell, Eugene and Carlotta O'Neill, Francis Parkman, Edgar Allan Poe statue, Walt Whitman, Malcolm X, William Lloyd Garrison, *Last Hurrah* movie still.

Used by permission of Orchard House/The Louisa May Alcott Memorial Association: Louisa May Alcott, Bronson Alcott, *Little Women* first edition frontispiece.

Courtesy of the Schlesinger Library, Radcliffe Institute, Harvard University: Lydia Maria Child, Frederick Douglass, Fannie Farmer, Margaret Fuller, Helen Keller with Annie Sullivan and Edward Everett Hale, Sara Josepha Buell Hale, Thomas Wentworth Higginson, Julia Ward Howe, William James, Sarah Orne Jewett, Elizabeth Peabody, Anne Sexton, Lucy Stone, Harriet Beecher Stowe, John Updike, John Greenleaf Whittier, "Looking up Beacon Street," Park Street Mall and Massachusetts State House, Louisburg Square, Radcliffe Yard.

Courtesy of Harvard University: W. E. B. Du Bois, Harvard Yard, John Harvard statue, Houghton Library, Memorial Hall, Widener Library (Rose Lincoln photograph).

Courtesy of the Boston Athenaeum: Annie Adams Fields, portrait by Lucia Fuller (gift of Mrs. E. Sturgis Hinds); Henry James; Amy Lowell; Cotton Mather, photo gravure by Goupil & Co., Paris, 1897, after the 1728 mezzotint by Peter Pelham; masthead from *The Liberator*; Washington Street, looking north from Water Street (Newspaper Row).

Courtesy of Houghton Mifflin Company: James T. Fields with Nathaniel Hawthorne and George Ticknor, Oliver Wendell Holmes, Sr., James Russell Lowell, Old Corner Bookstore.

Courtesy of Kahlil and Jean Gibran, © 1974: Kahlil Gibran, c. 1910.

Courtesy of the National Park Service, Longfellow National Historic Site: Nathaniel Hawthorne, Longfellow House.

Courtesy of the Concord Museum, Concord, MA: Central Concord, by J. W. Barber; title page of *Walden*.

Courtesy of the Concord Museum and the R. W. Emerson Memorial Association: Emerson's study (Nanlee Smith photograph).

From the collection of Minute Man National Historical Park, Concord, Massachusetts: Daniel Chester French's *Minute Man;* North Bridge.

From the archives of The Old Manse, a property of The Trustees of Reservations: Old Manse.

Index